Finger Moı

What you neε

Finger Monkey or Pygmy Marmoset Information

Pygmy Marmoset care, environment, behaviour, feeding and health.

by

Harry Holdstone

Table of Contents

Chapter 1: Introduction

The Pygmy Marmoset (*Cebuella pygmaea*) is not a very small marmoset but a distinct breed in its own right. These little creatures weigh in at 100 grams or $3^{1/}_{2}$ ounces and are the smallest True Monkey and the second smallest primate in the world. Their tiny size means that their 'cuteness' factor is off the chart! This is the reason for their popularity as pets.

The common or more popular names for these pint-sized primates are the Finger Monkey, Pocket Monkey, Dwarf Monkey or Little Lion. The first two arise from the fact that, especially as babies, these primates are so small they can cling to an adult human's finger.

Adult Pygmy Marmosets have golden-brown fur and are native to South America and the rainforests in the Amazon basin. They are found in areas where there are evergreen trees because they nest high in trees and they feed off tree gum.

Like most primates, this species lives in groups or troops. These social and family groups usually consist of between four and twelve individuals. The troop consists of the alpha or dominant male, his mate and their offspring. There may also be one or two individual males. All the troop members help to care for the babies in the group.

As with all True Monkeys, Pygmy Marmosets use a very sophisticated system of communication that involves sound, visual and scent or chemical signals. There is a wide range of vocal signals used to communicate with the other troop members.

While they are small and very appealing, these primates are *not* easy to care for. There are also several behavioural issues and aspects of caring for finger monkeys that are *not* pleasant to deal with. These will be discussed so that you know what you would have to contend with if you bought one of these exotic pets.

I hope that you find this book useful!

Chapter 2: Pygmy Marmoset basics

1) Geographic location and habitat

Pygmy Marmosets are native to several countries that have territory that falls within the western Amazon basin. Specifically, finger monkeys are indigenous or native to parts of Brazil, Bolivia, Columbia, Ecuador and Peru. The species is further divided into western and eastern Pygmy Marmosets.

Amazonas state in Brazil, South Colombia, North-Eastern Ecuador and Eastern Peru is home to the western marmosets or *Cebuella pygmaea pygmaea.* Its eastern counterpart, the *Cebuella pygmaea niveiventris*, is a resident of the Acre region of Brazil, Northern Bolivia and Eastern Peru.

Regardless of the country or region they live in, these tiny primates make their homes in bamboo thickets or in evergreen trees. They also live where their nests are close to water either in the form of a river or a plain that is subject to regular flooding. These marmosets will also always select a home in an area that offers cover and lots of places to hide and to feed. Trees satisfy both of these needs in abundance.

An entire troop or family group of Pygmy Marmosets requires very little territory; their range is usually smaller than half an acre in total size and consists of just a few trees off which they feed. They do not wander far and they do not require vast amounts of food.

These little monkeys don't nest or feed in the tree canopy or higher than 65 feet or 20 meters. They may be found on ground level but nest and feed higher up where they are safer from predators. The nests themselves are most often constructed at or towards the ends of branches. This makes it even harder for heavier predators to successfully reach them.

2) Personality

When describing the personality of the finger monkey it is rather similar to doing so for most primates and true monkeys. When one is specifically focussing on describing them as pets, the attributes or characteristics may shift.

The words that most owners and primate experts use include playful, smart and very demanding because they are extremely active. In addition, Pygmy Marmosets that have reached puberty and become mature adults have a reputation for being aggressive at times, unpredictable and destructive if their energy is not channelled correctly and they are not supervised.

These are not necessarily qualities one wants in a pet! They must be kept in mind when deciding whether or not to get a finger monkey especially if one doesn't have space, time and energy to provide the necessary care (including stimulation) and control.

3) Life span or expectancy

As with the majority of animals found in the wild and as pets, the life expectancy of Pygmy Marmosets depends on where they are.

In the wild these tiny true monkeys live for 11 or 12 years. If they are kept as pets or in zoos – and properly and well cared for – they may even reach the age of 18. This, too, must be kept in mind when considering having one as a pet: they are a long-term commitment!

4) Marmoset appearance and biology

Size and weight:

The measurements of the Pygmy Marmoset again demonstrate how diminutive these primates are.

Adults weigh between 85 and 140 grams or 3 to 5 ounces with an average weight of 3.5 ounces or 100 grams. Sexually mature females are slightly heavier than the males.

In terms of length, a Pygmy Marmoset's body (including its head) measures between 12 and 16 centimetres or 4.6 and 6.2 inches. Their tails are 6.8 to 9 inches or 17 to 23 centimetres long.

Colour and markings:

There is no difference in colouring or markings between male and female Pygmy Marmosets.

Their colour is hard to define as the fur on the head and back is a combination of brown, grey, orange, gold and black. The belly and underparts are lighter with tones of orange, yellow and tawny shades. What adds to the complexity is the fact that these primates have what is called agouti fur: each individual hair has brown and black stripes on it. This makes the fur look multi-coloured overall and provides these small marmosets with very good camouflage.

Both males and females have manes that surround the neck and face and cover the ears, flecks of white on the cheeks, a white vertical line between the eyes and black rings that run around their tails.

5) Special adaptations

There are several reasons why Pygmy Marmosets needed to develop special abilities and features:

(i)   They are very small and therefore vulnerable to predation

(ii)   They live in trees

(iii) They feed on a highly specialised diet: the gum from trees.

Each of these means that special adaptations are necessary so that these little primates can not only survive but thrive.

Sight:

Creatures that are small, weak and have a number of predators need to make up for what they lack in strength in other ways. The Pygmy Marmoset has a number of weapons in its arsenal.

Firstly, these primates have extremely good eyesight which they can utilise as they rotate their heads an astonishing 180 degrees! It's harder to sneak up on an animal that is able to do that, even from behind.

Teeth and digestion:

These marmosets have an unusual diet, which consists primarily of tree sap. In order to feed they need both specialised teeth and digestive systems.

In terms of their teeth, these primates have specially adapted and very sharp incisors on the lower jaw. They use them to gouge a hole in the bark of a tree. The gouging or up-and-down biting motion serves two purposes: it stimulates the flow of sap in the tree and it creates a little hole that sap collects in. Pygmy Marmosets then lap the sap out of this cavity using their delicate tongues.

Tree gum or sap is not an easily digestible substance. The digestive system of these primates has evolved to cope. They have a larger than normal cecum – a pouch-like structure between the small and large intestine – so that the food has more time to be broken down before being absorbed in the intestine.

Paws and claws:

The hands, fingers and nails found in Pygmy Marmosets are completely different to those in other primates.

They have claw-like nails – called *tegulae* – rather than flat fingernails that assist with climbing and clinging. In addition, their thumbs are not opposable, as they do not need to grasp or hold objects the way primates normally do.

Movement and locomotion:

Other true monkeys and primates have tails that they can use to grip and grasp branches. Pygmy Marmosets do not have this kind of prehensile tail because they use their claws for gripping and their tails to help with balance as they run headfirst up, down or along branches and leap from one branch, tree or vine to the next.

These little creatures are usually fairly slow, as this can help them to avoid detection by predators. However, when the need arises they can move very fast and, despite their size, make amazing leaps up to 5 metres or 16 feet to get out of trouble.

Size and deception:

These marmosets have one more trick up their sleeves: they fluff up their fur, which makes them appear larger and heavier than they are. This deters some predators who will think they will be harder to catch and eat than is in fact the case.

6) Pygmy Marmoset senses

These tiny primates have noteworthy sensory abilities, which help them to survive and thrive in their natural environment. The nature of these senses must be taken into consideration by owners in order to create a happy, healthy environment.

Vision

All male Pygmy Marmosets are red-green colour blind or dichromatic. This doesn't mean that they can't perceive colour but they see a limited colour palette. Reds, greens, browns and oranges all look very similar. Females may either be dichromatic or trichromatic (as most humans are) and therefore see a full range of colours and shades.

Their inability to distinguish certain colours should be kept in mind when one selects décor items for a captive habitat.

Hearing

Marmosets are able to hear sounds at very high frequencies and will pick up on – and make – high pitched noises. They also hear ultrasonic sounds that are beyond the abilities of the human ear.

The reason that this is important in relation to pet Pygmy Marmosets is that they will hear everyday sounds that their owner is oblivious to: the hum of lighting, the noise generated by computer monitors and televisions, cars and even the dripping of a leaking tap. These noises will not only be picked up but they may well become a source of stress, which may affect their health. Even sounds people find enjoyable such as music can be painful to the sensitive ears of primates.

Smell

Wild animals require an acute sense of smell in order to locate food, communicate, and warn them of the proximity of predators. Marmosets are one of the species that have specialised scent organs that also help them to pinpoint food with great accuracy and also use smell to determine the ripeness of fruit.

Touch

Not unusually, the sense of touch is thanks to billions of receptors in the skin that register pressure, texture, touch and even to temperature. While touch receptors are necessary for day-to-day activities, they have additional importance for Pygmy Marmosets.

Social relationships and bonds within the group are essential for the strength of the troop and the happiness and health of all the members. However, owners should note that while primates enjoy grooming each other and touching each other in various ways there is nothing to indicate that they find being touched by a human comparable or even enjoyable.

Taste

Taste helps primates locate and enjoy food. Providing foods that appeal to these primate's is very important.

7) Natural enemies and Predators

These tiny primates are not considered to be endangered. The International Union for Conservation of Nature has the species listed as "Least Concern". This designation means that conservationists consider these monkeys to be in no immediate risk of decline in numbers.

This doesn't mean the species does not face any risks. They fall victim to various species of wild cat, birds of prey such as eagles and hawks and to certain tree-climbing or dwelling snakes.

The two largest threats at this stage are the pet trade and the loss of their habitat due to deforestation and human encroachment.

Chapter 3: Behaviour

These marmosets might be small but their social structures and systems in the wild and within established troops are complex and fascinating. Unfortunately, it is unlikely that any private owner would be able to replicate the environment or establish a similar group and social system in captivity.

1) Social groups

A troop of Pygmy Marmosets ranges in size from 2 to 9 or even 12 individuals. The group members ordinarily consist of both 1 or 2 adult females and adult males. In addition, there will be one, or even two, generations of offspring of the breeding female. This means that a troop contains adults, sub-adults and young marmosets that are babies or juveniles.

These little primates share several activities within the group including rearing the young, watching for predators or danger and even sharing food. Both males and females care for the young in the group, regardless of who the parents are.

The juveniles also take part in rearing and seem to learn both parenting and rearing skills at a young age. In fact, it has been observed that young marmosets that have not been part of at least two troop rearing experiences make very poor parents or don't produce young.

2) Interaction within the group

Pygmy Marmosets enjoy the company of the other members of their troop. They engage in a behaviour that is common in primates generally: mutual grooming. This activity promotes bonding and social cohesion within the group.

Their interactions and the small size of the group allow them to form close bonds with each other. Researchers have even documented behaviour that indicates that these little primates experience sadness and distress when a member of their group dies.

Despite their generally easy-going nature with group members they will fight – to the death if necessary – to defend themselves and their group. While they usually get on very well and don't exhibit aggression towards each other in the wild, this can change in captivity.

Causes of aggression may be the lack of their normal or natural social structures or the fact that captivity is very stressful for them, especially if they were captured in the wild rather than bred in captivity. These disruptive factors may lead to atypical behaviour, which in turn could result in injuries and further stress.

3) Communication

These primates use a number of communication forms in order to interact with each other and neighbouring Pygmy Marmoset groups: vocal, visual and chemical signals. As with any other animal, communication serves to strengthen bonds, warn off rivals, signal readiness to mate and care for the young.

Vocal communications:

A number of studies have been done and they have revealed that Pygmy Marmosets produce no fewer than ten distinct sounds that they use to communicate with group members. The nature of the sound depends firstly on what is being communicated and, secondly, the distance the sound needs to travel.

While there are ten different sounds, there are three broad categories into which all calls fall: trills, whistles and clicks. Trills are used over both short and long distances to 'talk' to group members during feeding or foraging or when they are moving through their territory. Whistles and clicks are what are known as "alarm calls": they alert group members to danger or threats. The length of a call is determined by the distance between troop members.

If the call needs to cover only a short distance the sound will also be short. A longer or sustained call is used when members are further from each other. In addition, lower frequency calls are used when a greater distance must be covered as these sounds are less affected by vegetation, humidity and other sounds than high frequency noises.

In addition to warning of danger, calls are used to strengthen bonds, to initiate mating, to call or to encourage the young or to warn off members of neighbouring troops. These communications are called "contact calls".

Not only do Pygmy Marmosets understand what a call means, they also know exactly which troop member is producing it. The "what" and the "who" of a call both determine how the group or an individual will react to it. Of course these primates also know if the calls are coming from a marmoset that is not part of their troop.

Visual communications:

Visual displays are used by primates to show dominance, to indicate sexual receptiveness or when they feel threatened. For example, an arched back, strutting movements or bristling hair or fur (known as piloerection) are common signs of feeling threatened or showing dominance.

True monkeys, including Pygmy Marmosets, have very expressive faces and use their eyes, mouths, lips and eyelids to show emotions. Marmosets also use their manes as part of visual signals.

A mistake many people and primate owners make is to assume that all primate facial expressions correlate to our own. What one may think of as a smile may be lips drawn back by a primate that is feeling uncertain or even threatened or frightened.

An individual's body language must be observed to be correctly understood and interpreted. This is crucial for both the happiness of the Pygmy Marmoset and the safety of the owner.

Chemical or scent communications:

Glands located in the genital area and on the chest produce scents that are used for several purposes.

Males use the scent to mark out the troop's territory so that neighbouring groups stay away. Female Pygmy Marmosets use chemicals to signal to eligible males that she is in oestrus and able to produce young.

Body language:

Human beings have a tendency to interpret behaviour in animals in terms of their own. This can lead to misunderstandings, which can in turn result in a range of negative consequences.

For example, a primate with its lips drawn back and the teeth visible is not smiling or grinning. This is in fact an indication of fear; the primate is indicating submission. So, a primate that does this is not pleased to see its owner but feeling threatened.

4) Indicator behaviours

Certain behaviours should be looked for by Pygmy Marmoset owners or carers, as they are indications of both physical and emotional health or the lack of it. When negative indicators are observed, steps must be taken to address the problem or issues as soon as possible.

Positive indicators

Behaviours that indicate that the individual or individuals are doing well include:

✓ *Sharing food:* these tiny primates happily share food with other members of their troop. Even if an individual doesn't hand food to a companion, he or she will not object if a troop member takes food.

✓ *Self-grooming*: healthy, happy marmosets groom and keep themselves clean using both their mouths and hands.

✓ *Mutual grooming*: like many other primates, Pygmy Marmosets groom each other using their hands to comb through the fur of their companion. They may also 'nibble' each other's fur to remove dirt or parasites with their teeth.

They extend invitations to each other by lying down on their side or back next to the group member they want to be groomed by.

✓ *Nuzzling:* this is believed to be a social greeting. Finger Monkeys rub their muzzles against each other. The nuzzling may be against the face, body or anal area and may be accompanied by sniffing or licking or both.

Similar behaviour is observed in exchanges between other animals including domestic dogs and cats.

✓ *Hugging:* group members give each other body hugs using their arms just as other primates do. This is believed to be one of the bonding behaviours within troops. Hugs are often accompanied by nuzzling and / or licking.

✓ *Face licking:* while licking between adults takes place as part of bonding activities, it performs several important functions when it comes to infants.

Firstly – and obviously – it keeps the young clean. Secondly, it promotes bonding between the young and all the adult care givers and therefore improves overall group cohesion. Finally, researchers believe that licking the faces of marmoset babies stimulates them and improves their cognitive development.

✓ *Play:* Pygmy Marmosets engage in a great deal of energetic and boisterous play. Forms of play include somersaults, mock-biting, wrestling using their hands and / or feet, pouncing and patting. The patting, also referred to as batting, appears to be used to initiate play or some other kind of social interaction.

Solitary play and playing with others are both signs of a happy, healthy marmoset.

✓ *Wrestling:* Pygmy Marmosets engage in a great deal of energetic play. One form is wrestling where they use both hands and feet to grip each other and wrestle. There is no aggression in the wrestling and it never results in injuries.

✓

Negative indicators

If a Pygmy Marmoset is doing any of the following it's an indication that he or she is *not* well or happy and an intervention to address the situation is urgently required:

- *Low alertness:* if these tiny primates remain inactive or stationary and appear to be constantly vigilant, are sleeping far less and are 'jumpy', it's a sign that they are stressed and experiencing high levels of anxiety.

- *Agitated, rapid movement:* these little monkeys, unless they are running from danger or playing, usually move fairly slowly. Rapid walking, running, climbing or jumping from one place to another may well be an indication of stress or distress. These quick, sudden movements are usually accompanied by either an arched or extended tail.

- *Repetitive movements*: a marmoset in captivity that is repeatedly pacing, circling or weaving around or between the same objects is sending signals that its enclosure is too small and that it lacks space and stimulation.

- *Aggression and fighting:* as previously stated, Pygmy Marmosets are social and sociable little primates that get on well as a rule. However, if conditions in captivity are adverse this may change.

  Owners must be able to distinguish between playful behaviours and aggressive ones. Aggression manifests itself through chasing, hitting and / or biting. A bite that results in bleeding or a wound is never a playful nip. Aggressive bites are usually to the limbs or even the head.

- *Self-injurious activities and behaviour:* a marmoset that is hurting itself by pulling its hair, excessive scratching, biting itself, deliberately and repeatedly banging part of its head or body against an object or surface or any other action that results in injuries or the need for vet care are an indication of a serious problem that requires immediate resolution.

Indicators that are negative if the behaviour persists

Some behaviour is not at all problematic or of concern in and of itself. It does, however, become a problem if the behaviour continues rather than being an isolated or infrequent occurrence:

- o *Stealing food:* while it is common to see these primates sharing food, it is an indication of a problem if one animal snatches food from another and runs off with it. The marmoset who had food taken away may chase and this can escalate into an aggressive confrontation. While there is no cause for concern if this happens occasionally, if an individual steals often the situation must be investigated.

- o *Snapping / biting*: these are rapid, sharp bites and won't be mistaken for a nibble or a playful bite. These bites are also usually given on the neck area, which makes them potentially dangerous. Again this is only a worry if an individual bites others regularly.

- o *Cuffing*: while a quick cuff or smack is not unusual, especially when given to younger troop members to punish or teach it, this behaviour is a negative sign if the blows are frequent or particularly hard.

- o *Excessive scent marking*: while using scent is normal and captive Pygmy Marmosets scent mark more than those in the wild, if an individual rubs their belly or anal area on objects or surfaces very frequently it is a sign of stress, distress or a health issue.

- o *Presentation of the anal and genital area and tail*: usually a marmoset will raise its tail and present this area to another animal when it feels threatened or to show submissiveness.

  If this happens a great deal in relation to its human carer it indicates that the primate is feeling constantly fearful and under threat. This will have an impact on both the Pygmy Marmoset's behaviour and physical wellbeing.

5) The effect of environment on behaviour

The environment that is created for captive and pet Pygmy Marmosets has a profound effect on how these little primates behave. This is particularly the case with regards to social behaviour and interaction.

A poor environment leads to a marked decrease in a number of very important activities and behaviours: playing, grooming (self and mutual), scent marking and general levels of activity and movement. All of this affects bonding, the well-being of the group and the health of the individuals.

Furthermore, some studies have revealed that marmosets kept in a poor environment either have fewer offspring and / or are far more likely to suffer spontaneous abortions or miscarriages.

In light of this it must be stressed that captive environments for Pygmy Marmosets should reproduce their natural habitat as closely as possible in order to minimise the negative impact of an unnatural and restricted environment. The notion of habitat enrichment is therefore extremely important.

6) Foraging and feeding behaviour

Although most members of the troop care for the infants to some degree, the males in the group do the majority of the caring. This means that it is easier for females to feed because they are not carrying a baby or standing sentry at a nest. As a consequence, females are given priority when it comes to foraging. It is thought that this also helps the females recover after gestation, birth, lactating and feeding infants.

Gouging or gnawing on wood or stems is the way that Pygmy Marmosets in the wild gain access to the plant sap that they feed on. However, in a captive environment if a marmoset spends time gnawing and gouging and it does not produce food – or it is not necessary for food – the behaviour is a sign that the individual is stressed.

7) Interaction with people

Human beings and their activities affect the activity and the behaviour of Pygmy Marmosets in both the wild and in captivity. Both play and communication are necessary for healthy and happy troops and individuals, so this impact is of great concern.

The major effects are reduced play and vocal communication. In the wild these little primates become quieter when they are in close proximity to areas of human habitation. Captive marmosets are not only quieter but also produce a reduced range of types of call.

It may be that captive marmosets – understandably – see people as predators and this adversely affects the nature and range of their activities and interactions. This perception can lead to what is called mobbing behaviour: individuals in the group move towards and surround a would-be predator. This mobbing is accompanied by loud calls and even by aggressive behaviour and biting. If this is manifested often towards a pet owner it becomes a problem and even poses a health risk for both human and marmoset.

8) Biting

If one owns a primate or monkey – and that includes marmosets – one will be bitten. All primates bite and while a Pygmy Marmoset may not be able to bite as hard as a larger primate, the bite can still be serious in terms of behavioural and health implications.

The action a pet owner should take following a bite will depend on the circumstances and the type of bite. For instance a playful nip can be ignored, but an aggressive bite must be responded to so that the primate knows their owner is in charge. However, an owner should never make a primate fearful as that can lead to aggression.

There is a range of different bites that owners of primates will encounter and being able to differentiate is helpful:

> *Nibble*: a nibble or soft bite is also called an exploratory bite. The marmoset is examining, testing and tasting an object in order to decide if it can be eaten, played with or used in some way. It's a natural part of learning in babies who are exploring

and learning about their world. It's also common in young that are teething and have itchy, painful gums.

Nibbles are seldom painful and shouldn't be punished or even discouraged unless they continue for too long and begin to cause damage to items.

➢ *Play bite*: playful, non-aggressive bites are an important part of play for primates. It is similar to the play and gentle bites observed in puppies and kittens and there is never any intention of hurting or harming. There is no need to discipline a pet for a play-bite unless it is painful and begins to have an aggressive component.

A primate owner must decide what is an acceptable and then be consistent. In other words a bite that is painful should not be overlooked one day and then 'punished' the next.

➢ *Snap bites*: there is no mistaking this type of bite, as it is fast, painful and deep. These are aggressive bites and a pet primate can't be allowed to continue to give this type of bite, which often draws blood. A marmoset that gives a snap bite needs to be reminded by the owner that he or she is the dominant primate.

➢ *Multiple or repeat snap bites*: while a snap bite is usually followed by a retreat, some primates don't withdraw and go on to deliver a series of deep, painful bites. This indicates increased aggression and must not be tolerated by a pet owner.

➢ *Uninhibited bite*: these very nasty bites usually follow after a low, chattering warning sound. These bites are deep, deliberate and the primate clamps their jaw in place. With larger primates these bites may leave wounds that require stitches. This is less likely with Pygmy Marmosets but they can leave tears and punctures in the skin. A further reason these bites can be bad is that they are often aimed at the nose, face and ears. Stopping this behaviour once it has started is very difficult, even for an experienced primate owner.

It must be noted that having a primate's teeth removed as a way to stop biting is *not* an option – ever. It results in an inability to eat properly, facial deformities and an animal that loses trust in its owner and becomes fearful and unhappy.

Play and gentle biting should be allowed, as they are both natural and harmless forms of social interaction. However, bites that are about aggression or getting their own way must be managed and dealt with immediately and consistently. This must also be dealt with when the marmoset is still young or it becomes an intractable problem in an adult primate.

Some breeders suggest a little pinch on the bottom as a means of discipline. Others are appalled by the suggestion as they feel it could lead to injury in such a tiny creature, cause it significant pain and teach it nothing but fear!

The alternative these primate keepers recommend is shouting loudly ("No", "Stop" or just "Ouch!). This should be followed by a 3 to 5 minute 'time out' in its box or cage. Being deprived of interaction and stimulation is a punishment that a marmoset will not want repeated and he or she will make the association of 'naughty' bites and punishment quickly.

One can't ever stop biting altogether but one can prevent or at least seriously reduce the incidence of bites that are about getting what they want or hurting.

Chapter 4: Buying a Pygmy Marmoset

If one is still determined to buy a Pygmy Marmoset there are several issues one must keep in mind. It's important not to be swept away by how cute-looking these primates are or think that because they are small they don't need space and a great deal of attention.

1) Why these marmosets are not good pets

There are a number of factors that must be weighed against the appeal of these primates:

- ❖ These are wild animals and it is not possible to tame or domesticate them. They will never be self reliant and depend on their owner for everything.

- ❖ Given these marmosets can reach the age of 20 in captivity, so owning one is a long-term commitment that can't be undertaken lightly.

- ❖ Baby Pygmy Marmosets require feeding every two hours for the first 2 weeks. That's a very tough ask for most pet owners. Hand rearing is a difficult job that requires patience, time and energy.

- ❖ These little marmosets are not easy to care for and they require the services of a vet who has primate experience.

- ❖ After they reach sexual maturity these primates often become unpredictable and aggression is not uncommon. In fact, they have reputations as biters.

- ❖ A further drawback is that one can't only have one Finger Monkey, as they must live in groups. Even if one has more than one of these primates it is still essential to give them time and energy.

- ❖ They require constant mental stimulation and will demand it very loudly and strenuously if it isn't forthcoming.

- They are expensive to buy (again, one can't only have a single pet) and setting up the correct habitat and caring for them is also costly.

- Despite their small size they require a large enclosure and a range of toys and other objects that will provide mental stimulation.

- In some countries a license or permit is required in order to own a Pygmy Marmoset. In others, primates in general are not permitted. It should be noted that at time of writing South America had banned the export of these little creatures and North America had outlawed their import.

- A habit that captive marmosets develop is throwing their faeces at the other marmosets and / or their owner or simply playing with their excrement.

- Their cage or enclosure can't be kept inside, as the odour is most unpleasant. Their urine is very pungent – especially the male's – and they urinate often including on their own hands as it aids with climbing.

- Captive marmosets are also known to urinate on their owners in order to scent mark them as part of their territory.

- Their enclosures or cages must be thoroughly cleaned and disinfected weekly.

- They are extremely difficult to train even for experienced primate owners and handlers.

- Pygmy Marmosets are prone to a number of common illnesses, many of which they catch from people because they affect humans too. For example, they can contract chickenpox, measles, HIV and cold sores. While a cold sore is painful and unsightly in a human, this herpes virus is fatal for these tiny primates.

   To make this even more complex, people can catch illnesses from marmosets too. Cross-contamination is common unless preventative steps are taken.

- ❖ If a Pygmy Marmoset feels emotionally neglected they will let their owner – and anyone else in close proximity or earshot – know. These unhappy primates will bite, throw things, hurt themselves and scream in order to get the attention and stimulation they crave. Even if an owner can handle these behaviours, many neighbours won't.

2) More reasons why marmosets aren't good pets

Yes, these points are being repeated but it is necessary to do so in order to ensure that any potential primate owner fully understands the unique challenges and demands of these pets. This is for the Pygmy Marmoset's sake and that of the owner!

- All primates, including these tiny marmosets, are wild animals. With patience, love, training and discipline these little critters may become friendly, even affectionate, but they will *never* be tame.

- Wild animals, including primates, are not pets but rather animals that the owner has created a habitat for. They are a long-term commitment and far more costly and considerably more demanding than a conventional, true pet could ever be.

- With the best will in the world, and all the patience one can muster, a primate can't be toilet trained. Like other wild animals they will, with the exception of their nests, urinate or defecate wherever they happen to be when the urge strikes.

- Training has limited success and must continue throughout a primate's life. They may not learn at all and, if they do, it will not happen fast. While primates are smart they have no desire to please their owner the way a pet does so this motivation to learn is absent. Marmosets will do what they want to do, when they want to do it.

- As discussed in the previous section, all primates bite. This natural behaviour can't and shouldn't be stopped, although more severe biting must and can be discouraged. Primates can also be unpredictable and so bites can happen without warning.

- Their unpredictability, speed and tendency to bite mean they are not suitable pets to have around young children (who can be unpredictable too).

- Marmosets are not good around other pets as a rule, although some will be okay with cats and dogs if they are gentle and docile. Pygmy Marmosets will find large birds very frightening.

- They must have company; optimally they need to be part of a Pygmy Marmoset group. At the absolute minimum they need regular, dedicated interaction with their owner.

  Because of the demanding nature of these animals, one can't just use the services of a pet sitter if one goes away or works long hours. One needs someone with primate experience. Finally, the bond with one's marmoset will be broken by frequent and / or extended time away. Once broken, trust can be very hard to re-establish.

- Again because they demand attention, and they generate a great deal of work, having marmosets as pets devours one's free time almost completely.

  The owner of a primate, especially one that is allowed time in the home, will be spending his or her time preparing food, feeding, cleaning up mess of various kinds (excrement, shredded paper or fabric, broken objects, spills or various kinds, washing or changing nappies) or looking for items that have been stolen or lost by a curious, playful primate. As an owner one just has to deal with all of this... every day.

- Primate owners who allow their pets to be in the house can't display plants or vases of flowers unless he or she is okay with having them destroyed or eaten. Books, magazines and fabrics will get tatty and stain-covered in no time at all, as will cushions, pillows and anything else that can be tasted, chewed or played with. Ornaments must be under lock and key if they are breakable.

- Even Pygmy Marmosets that live in clean enclosures and sleep in clean bedding will smell. All types of primates smell: a musky, slightly sweet odour that is far from pleasant.

- These little primates are very expensive both initially and on an ongoing basis: enclosure décor, nappies, food, medical care, toys etcetera.

3) Are you really a suitable marmoset owner?

It's not only a case of "Is this the pet for me" but "Am I the right kind of person to own a marmoset?" A prospective marmoset owner should have certain characteristics, traits, knowledge and abilities. One needs to:

✓ Be prepared to educate oneself about Pygmy Marmosets specifically and primates generally.

✓ Be mature, patient, calm (even under pressure or when provoked) and possess a high tolerance threshold for frustration, mess and noise.

✓ Have the financial and emotional resources that are necessary to care for a primate.

✓ Spend a large proportion of time at home so that the pet marmoset is not left caged and or alone for extended periods.

✓ Put the marmoset's needs first. The owner and his or her needs, interests, friends and so forth must take a back seat as a primate pet must take priority.

✓ Be mature and assertive. A primate owner needs to be able to assert their dominance and not lose their cool when faced with mess or even when bitten. All crises must be handled calmly and maturely. Negative behaviour must be dealt with immediately and firmly. If a primate owner becomes fearful or hesitant he or she loses their status as the alpha and the primate's negative behaviour will escalate.

✓ Handle mess and bad smells without being squeamish. A marmoset, unless it is wearing a nappy, is going to leave excrement where it goes and may also smear it around (on purpose or by accident). The owner needs to patiently and constantly clean up after their primate child to keep it and its environment clean and as hygienic as possible.

4) Tips on selecting a healthy Finger Monkey

If one still wants a Pygmy Marmoset there are things one should be on the lookout for. There are a number of features and factors that will help one to assess the health of a marmoset. It's necessary to spend time observing a marmoset in order to establish its state of health and mind.

- o Healthy, glossy coat with no signs of hair loss or balding patches.

- o Clear and shiny eyes with no signs of discharge or opaqueness to the iris.

- o The marmoset is alert and shows an active interest in the world around it.

- o The tail should be long and mobile with no signs of injury.

- o The animal is energetic; lethargy is an indicator of illness in these energetic little critters.

- o It interacts with the other marmosets in a relaxed, easy manner: mutual grooming, sharing of food, playing and cuddling behaviours are shown.

- o It does not display aggression towards the other primates or its handler.

- o Its movements are relaxed and smooth and fairly slow, except during play.

- o It does not appear anxious or overly vigilant.

- o The marmoset does not act fearfully when handled by a human.

5) How to tell females and males apart

Differentiating between infant males and females is not easy based on overall appearance. It is, however, easier with juvenile Pygmy

Marmosets, as genital differences become apparent. With mature or adult marmosets the females are a little heavier than the males.

6) One, two or more

There is no debate amongst owners who are primate experts on this matter: a solitary marmoset is a lonely and unhappy one.

These social and gregarious primates need each other and *must* have the companionship of at *least* one other Pygmy Marmoset. Preferably they should live in a group as they do in the wild. This is a large part of reproducing natural conditions as closely as possible.

Furthermore, it is far better to have more than one social group. Firstly, young marmosets – especially young males – leave the group in the wild. If they can't do so it can lead to greatly increased aggression and frequent fights to establish dominance. In addition, if there is only one group – in particular a small group – the death of one of the members has a far more profound effect on the other members of the troop.

The bottom line in terms of how many Pygmy Marmosets one should own is that a solitary primate will be desperately miserable. An unstable troop will have stressed members. A primate that is unhappy is likely to become depressed, withdrawn and even ill or destructive, needy and aggressive. As a primate owner one has a responsibility to achieve, promote and maintain the health and happiness of the animals in one's care.

Chapter 5: What Pygmy Marmosets need

1) The cage / enclosure

The cage or enclosure that pet Pygmy Marmosets live in must provide all that is necessary for their well-being. In broad terms, the environment must help to keep these little primates healthy or disease free and allow them to enact and retain natural behaviours and skills including foraging, playing, grooming and so forth.

As with most species, health and happiness in captive finger monkeys are closely linked. Stressed or unhappy animals, for instance, are far more likely to become sick as their immune system becomes weak.

In other words, the captive environment must reproduce as closely as possible the natural habitat. This applies to the objects and features such as plants and tree branches and to the space and wherewithal to exhibit natural behaviours such as climbing and foraging.

While it's not possible to completely accurately assess how happy a pet primate is, the best indicator is its behaviour. If what a Pygmy Marmoset does in captivity is very close to they way it would behave if it was still living wild then that's a good indicator that it's happy. Not only should the behaviours be very similar or the same but captive primates should spend about as much time each day engaging in the various activities as their counterparts in the wild do.

In terms of size and the nature of an enclosure or cage, these little marmosets need considerably more space than their size would lead one to believe. One has two options: a very large cage / enclosure or a smaller cage that is attached to a very large exercise area. The minimum size for a cage or enclosure is 3 x 3 x 4 feet or 1 x 1 x 1.2 metres (height x depth x width). However, other primate owners state that an enclosure should be at least 6 x 3 x 6 feet or 1.9 x 0.95 x 1.9 metres in size. The width is important, as marmosets leap and jump from point to point and they need height for climbing and nesting.

The primary reason why an indoor cage is *not* a good idea is that Pygmy Marmosets can be very smelly… and noisy. If one doesn't have outdoor space to use one should either be truly rigorous about cleaning or get another kind of pet.

Outdoor cages and enclosures have additional requirements. Pet Pygmy Marmosets must have protection from the elements and areas where they can sun themselves and obtain vitamin D3 (these rays don't penetrate glass). The enclosure must also be temperature controlled during the cold months and secure so that they can't escape and they can't be stolen or bothered by people or animals.

2) Furnishings / décor

This is where one needs to replicate the natural habitat as much as possible so that the captive primates are happy and healthy. There are a number of items that must be provided:

- *Branches*: natural branches must be used and, if possible, there should be a lot of them. The branches must be positioned at a range of different angles and offer a variety of textures, diameters and degrees of flexibility. This will allow these little primates to grip, climb, leap and cope with surfaces that react differently to movement and weight. This goes a very long way to ensuring these primates retain all of their important locomotion skills.

    Owners of these little primates suggest that the majority of the branches should be positioned well above ground height. In the wild, Pygmy Marmosets nest and forage in the upper branches. However, a few branches can be positioned closer to the ground as captive marmosets do drop to the ground to forage for food that has been dropped.

- *Foliage:* foliage is a very important component when it comes to creating a marmoset habitat. In an outdoor enclosure one can incorporate live trees and shrubs. It is not possible to do so to the same degree in an indoor enclosure. However, one can include potted plants and trees. It is crucial that one ensure that none of the plants used, either indoors or outdoors, are toxic for primates!

The foliage serves several functions: it provides cover and privacy, affords protection from the elements, adds to the interest of the overall environment and it also attracts insects, which can be hunted and eaten.

- *Ropes*: these are useful to simulate vines and creepers, which may be used as these little animals climb or leap about in the enclosure.

- *Nest box*: Pygmy Marmosets feel much safer if they can sleep and nest high up in branches and in an enclosed space like a box or nest box. They enjoy having a blanket or towel inside the box to snuggle into.

  It's also a good idea, if one has a group of these primates, to set up a second nest box just in case an individual is being bullied or not allowed to join the others in the primary nest box. He or she will then have a shelter to use.

- *Substrate / floor covering:* with outdoor enclosures grass is a very good natural, absorbent ground cover. For indoor cages or enclosures one needs something that is functional and easy to remove. Options include several layers of newspaper, woodchips, peat, sawdust or – a far more costly one – puppy pads.

- *Perches and platforms:* these tiny primates need stable places where they can sit or perch while they feed and when they use their sharp incisors to gouge holes in the branches in their cage. This biting and gouging is an important natural behaviour and it helps to keep their gums and teeth healthy.

Every aspect of furnishings is very important, as it plays a part in creating an environment that is fairly close to the natural habitat of Pygmy Marmosets. All of them can also be used to supply a further aspect that is crucial for these lively, curious primates: stimulation. A responsible owner will change the environment – for example, move or add branches or foliage – now and then so that new exploration and play opportunities become available.

3) Lighting

As previously mentioned, all primates need vitamin D3 but marmosets require much more of this vitamin than other primates do. A deficiency can lead to nutritional and subsequently health issues. The best source of D3 is natural sunlight.

If one is unable to have an outdoor enclosure or lives in a location with limited sunshine and warm weather then it is essential to expose captive Pygmy Marmosets to ultraviolet light every day. In order to do so one should install full-spectrum fluorescent lights very close to the enclosure or cage. Because these lights lose the efficacy over time it is suggested that they should be replaced twice a year.

4) Temperature and humidity

These primates come from an environment with moderate heat and humidity. A captive habitat needs to replicate these conditions.

- *Temperature*: The range required is 70 – 80° Fahrenheit or 21 – 27° Celsius. This can be achieved by using carefully placed sunlamps. However, it is crucial that the lamps are not positioned where the marmosets can reach them as they could burn themselves. The heat sources should also not be placed too close to live plants, as the leaves can be scorched.

  Areas in the cage or enclosure should allow 'sunbathing' and outdoor enclosures must also include areas of shade in the hot months.

  One must invest in a reliable thermometer to measure the temperature in the habitat to ensure that it remains within the necessary range.

- *Humidity*: The humidity levels for Pygmy Marmosets should be between 40 and 60%. It is easier to generate and maintain humid conditions in outdoor enclosures as a moist flooring material or substrate such as soil or peat can be used.

  One can invest in a humidifier to generate the necessary moisture in the air. However, having a damp substrate or other sources of moisture in the enclosure is also effective. The higher temperatures these primates need will cause some evaporation and the moisture particles will be suspended in the air.

A hygrometer – which can be purchased from a pet store or online – will measure the humidity levels so that one can see that they stay within range.

5) Feeder and water container

Food and feeding is discussed in more detail in chapter 7, but in terms of utensils and locations, Pygmy Marmosets require sturdy food bowls and many enjoy having a large, flat food platform at which they can feed. They will only venture to the floor of the cage to forage for any pieces of food that may have been dropped.

Like all animals, Pygmy Marmosets need a constant source of clean drinking water. They do best, though, when they are supplied with water bottles and / or sipper tubes that are placed at heights where they are easy to drink from. Ordinary water bowls are not suitable, and may even pose a drowning risk with the babies, for these little creatures.

6) Other important equipment

In addition to the various décor items already discussed, there are various items you will need in order to prepare for and care for your pet marmoset. They include:

- Blankets or towels for inside the nesting boxes
- Food bowls
- Feeding bottles and / or sipper tubes and bottles
- Poop-scoop to help clean up faeces
- An implement that is suitable for cleaning out the bottom of the cage or enclosure
- Humidifier
- Heat lamps
- Thermometer to monitor the temperature in the habitat
- Hygrometer to monitor the humidity in the habitat
- Toys (more on these in chapter 6).

7) *A starter kit for a new – and first – baby marmoset*

Some breeders supply or sell a "starter kit" to their clients along with a baby Pygmy Marmoset.

Food items

The primary food item is *low iron* baby formula. Too much iron causes serious liver problems, and even failure, which results in death. One can also purchase callitrichid (marmoset and tamarin) food, which is higher in D3, calcium and vitamin C than other commercial primate foods. Natural grain cereals are also very useful when one reaches the stage of moving to solid foods.

Equipment

A feeding syringe (or two) is essential. These syringes make measuring quantities easy and they have soft silicone nipples on the end rather than a hard plastic tip. This makes it easy for the infant to suckle from them.

If one is going to go down the nappy route, one must do so from the beginning. It is possible to purchase marmoset nappies in a range of sizes for both infants and adults. While cloth napkins are recommended by many breeders they do require very thorough washing, rinsing and drying. Disposable ones are far less work but much more costly.

Wipes are also necessary if nappies are going to be used. They help to clean tiny bottoms between nappy changes. It is essential that one only uses a brand and type that will not cause a bad reaction or toxicity in primates. Hypoallergenic baby wipes are probably safe.

While adult marmosets are happy to cuddle into blankets or towels and with each other in nesting boxes, an infant that is being hand-reared needs something to snuggle into and sleep in when he or she is not being carried by its owner. One can purchase a number of items including 'pockets', bags and sleep sacks. Many of these are sheepskin or faux sheepskin-lined and help to keep the infant warm. They also give the baby something to cling to for security and comfort.

Chapter 6: Caring for a Pygmy Marmoset

As with any pets, and especially exotic pets, these primates rely on their owner for everything. Owning one or a group of marmosets is a huge responsibility that encompasses a number of aspects.

1) Stimulation

One reason why Pygmy Marmosets and other primates are desirable pets is because they are very intelligent and full of energy. While these are certainly lovely qualities to have in a pet they do mean that an owner has to make sure that there is enough stimulation to keep these little critters busy and happy. A bored, unhappy primate is a destructive primate and this in turn leads to a very unhappy and stressed owner!

To overcome this it is necessary to create a habitat that contains branches and platforms to explore and climb, lots of toys to play with, swings and / or hammocks and, if space permits, tunnels. The most important, though, is the presence of at least one other Pygmy Marmoset.

A solitary primate will require far more play and interaction with its owner and may become needy and demanding. In addition, some owners say that the cage should be near something that provides interest and can be watched such as a television, bird cage, aquarium or a window. This will help to alleviate some of the boredom and loneliness the primate experiences while its human companion is away.

Marmosets explore and examine every inch of their habitat. After a fairly short while this will lose its appeal, as they will know their environment so well. For this reason one should make changes weekly. These alterations should be significant enough to create new interest for the pet but not so marked that the changes to the habitat are experienced as threatening or stressful.

2) Attention, affection and supervision

Pygmy Marmosets need constant entertainment and mental stimulation. This is, as previously stated, especially true of a solitary primate. The owner becomes the entire source of companionship, affection, play and intellectual challenges.

These little animals *need* cuddles, play and interaction. If they don't get it they will demand it… loudly, incessantly and in dramatic fashion. If an individual is not willing or is not in a position to give a marmoset a great deal of time he or she should quite simply *not* have one of these primates as a pet. Pygmy Marmoset owners must be able and willing to function as their pet's troop and supply all the things that other marmosets and a life in the wild would provide.

A Finger Monkey that is emotionally neglected will seek the attention it craves and the resultant behaviour can be very destructive and distressing. These little primates will scream shrilly, loudly and constantly, pull out their hair, scratch themselves, bite, hit themselves and even have fits.

This behaviour is not only impossible to ignore, but it should not be ignored as it is a sign of huge stress and distress and will result in injury, illness and damage to property. It is also stressful for an owner and it is his or her responsibility to deal with the situation immediately.

Even in optimal circumstances – in other words where there is more than one happy, healthy Pygmy Marmoset and more than one troop or group – these primates should not be allowed the run of the house without very close supervision. The reason is not because they are by nature naughty or destructive but that they are smart; curious; fast runners, climbers and leapers and they love boisterous play. In the course of all of this spirited activity things get broken, 'stolen' and unless your marmosets wear nappies they will also leave urine and faeces in their wake.

3) Nappies / diapers

Nappies are a less fun part of owning a Pygmy Marmoset. They may not need to wear them in their cage or enclosure but a nappy is essential if they are in one's home or the owner doesn't wanted to get urinated or defecated on.

What type is best?

The most significant point is that one must use nappies or diapers that are specifically designed for primates. These accommodate the placement of the back legs and the tail. At time of writing there were several online stores supplying primate nappies in every size in order to cater for infants and adults. Many owners prefer to use cloth nappies that are washable and reusable. The primary reasons are cost and safety. Firstly, disposable nappies are expensive and they become an ongoing expense. Secondly, disposable nappies can be ripped up and if pieces of the padding or stuffing are ingested they can cause choking or an obstruction on the primate's digestive system.

Nappies that are impregnated with some sort of chemicals and gels should also be avoided as they can cause adverse skin reactions.

It is very important to ensure that the nappy fits extremely well for a number of reasons: so that it doesn't leak, it can't be pulled off easily by the marmoset and, finally, so that it is harder for tiny hands to get into the diaper and dig around in it.

4) Cleaning

Given Pygmy Marmosets scent-mark their territory very frequently and will urinate and defecate pretty much anywhere except in their nest boxes, it's essential to clean and disinfect their cages regularly. With an indoor cage a weekly clean will be necessary or the smell will become overwhelming. However, in an effort not to cause these little primates stress, cause them to become 'disorientated' or start scent-marking even more frequently, one should clean and disinfect the cage in sections. In other words, one shouldn't clean the entire cage at the same time. Also, a mild disinfectant must be used. One should check with someone who is knowledgeable about which brands would be best, as some chemicals will be toxic for marmosets.

When cleaning the cage it is important not to overlook the nest boxes, food platforms and the branches all of which must be cleaned well.

5) *Training*

As with any animal it is important to start training as soon as possible. Most primates can begin training when they are six to eight weeks old. It's also crucial that one begins with realistic expectations and bears in mind that:

- It will be very, very slow going and will require a huge amount of patience and restraint.

- Most marmosets will never be successfully trained.

- Although primates are very smart they are not motivated to learn and perform the way dogs are, for instance. Pleasing their owner is not part of their thinking at all. They will only do what benefits them and what they want to do, when they want to do it.

- One can't ever domesticate or tame any kind of primate, including marmosets.

The key to training, however, is to use rewards or positive reinforcement. As stated, a primate will do something that pleases it or results in something pleasing. So, work out what your Pygmy Marmosets enjoy and use it – whether it is a healthy snack / treat or play time – to reward good or desirable behaviour. This way a primate associates doing something, or not doing something, with a reward or something it enjoys.

Failure to perform the desirable behaviour should not be punished – ever. Punishment only teaches anxiety and fear which can manifest as ill health or aggression or both. Failure to perform the desired behaviour or action should simply not be rewarded.

Some primate owners suggest one should give a marmoset a small pinch on the fleshy part of a buttock to discourage negative behaviour that can't be allowed to continue such as biting.

6) Protecting your Finger Monkey from toxic plants

Primate owners are sometimes tempted to buy plants for a primate enclosure because they look lush or even pretty. If a pet marmoset has the run of the house then pot plants are a potential source of danger too. The following are poisonous if touched: Rubber Plants, Primrose, Poinsettia, Milkweed, Poison Oak and Ivy, thistles and nettles. Some of these may germinate in an outdoor enclosure after seeds have blown in. Pet owners need to be vigilant for plants that grow out of the enclosure substrate. The list of plants that are toxic if ingested is far longer. However, only those likely to be found as pot plants or part of floral arrangements or seasonal decorations are listed here:

- Azaleas
- Daffodils
- Dieffenbachia
- Holly
- Mistletoe
- Lupines
- Hyacinth
- Impatiens
- Lilly of the Valley
- Narcissus
- Philodendron
- Rhododendron
- Sweet Pea
- Poinsettia
- Cyclamen
- Delphinium
- Elephant Ear Plant
- Foxgloves
- Hydrangeas
- Ivy
- Tulip.

This list names plants that are commonly found in homes but it must be noted that it is not exhaustive. If one is unsure about the safety of a plant or plant part, one must check with a primate vet or care centre.

Chapter 7: Feeding your pet Marmoset

1) Feeding in the wild

While the primary food of Pygmy Marmosets is tree sap, gum or resin (collectively know as tree exudate), they enjoy a varied diet in the wild. Plant exudate provides them with most of carbohydrates, calcium and protein that they require. Their diet is supplemented by fruit, flower nectar, insects, very small reptiles and other plant matter. This is particularly the case if sap or gum is scarce for some reason.

Obtaining gum or sap from trees is time consuming and requires a lot of effort and patience. Once holes have been gnawed in the bark of the vine or tree, the marmoset must wait for the resin to ooze out so they can lap it up. Time is also spent hunting for insects and foraging for fruit and edible plant matter. It is estimated that some 50% of their day is spent looking for food and feeding. Most foraging and feeding is done by marmosets in the wild during the early morning and the earlier part of the afternoon.

Just as people have favourite eating places, so do Pygmy Marmosets. It has been observed that both groups and individuals favour certain trees. They keep returning to that tree – or those trees – and, over time, they will gnaw literally hundreds of holes in the bark. If a tree begins to yield less sap, the troop or individual will transfer its attention to another tree. This means that the marmosets get the sustenance they need and the tree has a chance to recover. Animals are instinctively good at ensuring sustainability, unlike human beings.

2) What to feed adult marmosets in captivity

The diet of captive Pygmy Marmosets must mirror the diet of those in the wild as closely as possible. This applies not only to the nature of the food but also to feeding behaviours such as gnawing, lapping and foraging.

Just like their free counterparts, pet marmosets need a varied diet that must not only meet their nutritional requirements but also look and smell appealing and taste good. As with any other living creature, the correct foods are essential to ensure overall health, resistance to disease and stress, normal growth, longevity and the ability to reproduce. Pygmy Marmosets also require foods that are very high in vitamins C and D3. These little primates are prone to problems with weight (both overweight and underweight) and with their teeth. The correct, balanced diet can prevent this.

It's important *not* to give primates the same food day after day. They will become bored and lose interest in food, which will impact on their health and general well-being. Fortunately there is a wide range of foods that one can give to captive marmosets to keep their diets interesting.

This means a lot of work for the owner as food must be sourced, purchased, chopped, cooked and so on. One can't feed these tiny creatures any food or items that pose a choking hazard; all food must be chopped fine or be soft enough for marmosets to bite, tear and chew with ease.

Pygmy Marmosets should be fed several times or at least twice a day. Food should be placed in several different locations so that they have to look for food or forage as they would in the wild and each marmoset gets food. Food bowls and platforms should be placed in branches and high in the cage. These tiny primates feel safer at this height and it is not natural for them to feed at ground level, although they may do some ground level foraging.

In broad terms the recommended diet for marmosets in captivity can be broken down as follows:

- 75 – 80%: commercial Marmoset food (this can be dried and or tinned food)
- 15 – 20%: vegetables, fruit, whole grains, seeds, nuts or other plant material
- 5 – 10%: protein
- 2 – 5%: insects.

The protein required by these primates can be obtained from a range of ordinary foods such as chicken (the white meat), fish and hard boiled eggs. The fish and chicken must be boiled, poached or grilled.

Insects that are popular with Pygmy Marmosets include small beetles, crickets, wax worms and meal worms. Captive marmosets will have great fun hunting live insects. However, if one is concerned that the 'food' might escape and get into one's home then dead, dried insects can also be used. Any flies, small reptiles such as lizards or spiders that wander into the cage or enclosure will also be enjoyed as snacks.

Given that all insects are very high in protein, they should only be given as part of a meal or as a treat or snack once a week and not daily in addition to other protein sources. Too much protein is not good for most primates.

The good news is that one doesn't have to harvest tree exudate of some sort for marmosets; one can purchase suitable tree sap or gum from specialist pet shops and online.

They also enjoy eating whole grains such as rice, seeds, nuts and oatmeal included in their diets. If one can lay one's hands on fresh, tropical flowers these little monkeys will lick all the nectar out of them and love every second of it.

A regular feeding schedule would look something like this:

➢ *Daily*:

- Specially formulated commercial marmoset food
- Chopped fruit
- Fresh vegetables
- Cooked vegetables
- Rice
- Baby cereal
- The white of a hardboiled egg
- Cooked fish or the white meat from a chicken or turkey
- Vitamin supplements (this is especially important if the marmosets get very little or no natural sunlight).

Remember that all fruit must be washed carefully to remove any pesticides or other chemicals from the skin.

➤ *Twice weekly*:

- A variety of both live and dried insects
- Multivitamins.

One of the best ways to mimic feeding in the wild is by making Arabic gum, which is rich in various important minerals including calcium and an excellent source of energy. There are several recipes for making up an Arabic Gum – which is readily available in-store and online – solution. The most popular ones are:

- 70% clean, unfortified water + 30% gum powder
- 70% pure fruit juice + 30% gum powder.

One can also sprinkle Arabic Gum powder over chopped fruit.

3) Food delivery methods or systems

Given that in the wild these little primates are hunters and foragers, feed off tree gum and sap, and prefer to feed above ground level, owners must replicate these behaviours and conditions as closely as possible. There are a number of things one can do to achieve this:

✓ Drill holes into the branches or bamboo poles in the enclosure or cage and use a syringe to inject Arabic gum solution into the holes so the marmosets can lap it out.

✓ Release live insects into the cage or enclosure twice a week so the marmoset(s) can hunt and catch them.

✓ Place feeding platforms and bowls (heavy ceramic or dog food bowls work well) above ground level where these little primates feel safe.

✓ Place food in more than one place in the cage or enclosure. This is essential if one has more than one group or troop sharing an enclosure; each group requires their own feeding area.

- ✓ Suspend fruit from branches or skewer them on the ends of sticks where they can be reached without any danger of the primates becoming entangled or injured.

- ✓ Captive marmosets will be encouraged to move around and forage more if some dry food is lightly scattered on the cage or enclosure floor. It should be noted, however, that some primate experts are opposed to this because ground level foraging is not a natural behaviour for Pygmy Marmosets.

4) How to feed babies

Hand-rearing of infant marmosets is difficult and demanding and will be discussed in greater detail in a later chapter of this guide.

At this point it should be noted though that babies should never be fed when they are lying on their backs. They must be lying on their tummies with their heads tilted slightly and gently back. This will remove the very real danger of choking, food aspiration (regurgitating and then inhaling food particles) and death.

5) Drinks

Your Pygmy Marmoset must have adequate fluid intake in order to remain healthy. Given they feed twice a day and may snack in between 'meals' they get thirsty and therefore must have constant access to water.

The water one provided for primates must be clean, unfortified (in other words it must not be fortified with chemicals such as fluoride as some tap water is) and not too cold.

In terms of containers, one should use a heavy bowel that can't be knocked over easily. The container must also not be so large that it poses a drowning risk if a baby fell in. One could also invest in one of the models of drinking fountains available at pet stores and online.

If one wants to provide a treat or some variety, water can be supplemented with diluted, organic fruit juice (not fruit juice concentrate), goat's milk, milk formula (the type used for babies) or even almond milk. Soy products should be avoided, as there have been reports of an increase in aggression levels in adult marmosets that were given these products.

6) Food enrichment

This should more accurately be termed "feeding enrichment" rather than "food enrichment" as it refers to making the activity of feeding as natural and enjoyable for marmosets as possible.

What one feeds primates and how one presents the food needs to allow and encourage their natural feeding behaviours. With Pygmy Marmosets this involves feeding in such as way that they are encouraged to gnaw, gouge, forage, climb, lap, hunt and catch, leap and reach in order to feed. This is why using live insects and suspending fruit, for example, are very effective enrichment strategies.

Food enrichment does not refer to providing additional food or treats. Marmosets can become overweight rather easily.

7) Supplemental feeding

Pygmy Marmosets, and other marmosets, are not able to produce Vitamin A (also known as vitamin D3). This vitamin is essential for healthy bones and must be provided as a supplement, particularly for captive marmosets that have little or no regular exposure to natural sunlight.

One can purchase D3 in either liquid or powder form, either of which can be added to food. It is essential to read the directions and not to give too much of this supplement as it can reach toxic levels. As a general guide, a single drop or a light sprinkle of powder twice or three times a week should be sufficient.

It's also advisable to give marmosets one quarter of a 250 mg chewable Vitamin C tablet. Administering this is not difficult, as primates appear to enjoy the taste. These tablets can be easily obtained from pharmacies and most supermarkets.

8) Treats

Like most primates, Pygmy Marmosets have a sweet tooth. It's alright to give these little creatures the odd sweet treat. They enjoy marshmallows, fruit gums, jelly, liquorice, cake and biscuits. The important thing is not to be so seduced by the delight of a marmoset eating a treat that one gives him or her too much.

All of these sweet items must be strictly rationed: a *very* small piece as a reward as part of training or, if they are a regular treat, once or maximum twice a week.

9) What NOT to feed your finger monkey

There are a number of things that should not be fed to Pygmy Marmosets, only because they cause weight gain and may also lead to dental problems. Most of the sweet treat items fall into this category so it is worth repeating that while you can give your pet a small piece of, for instance, marshmallow it must be just that: small and one piece only. And one can't give in to begging, tantrums and so forth. Marmosets have no self-control so the owner must control what their pet consumes.

Grapes and *chocolate* are both enjoyed by these primates but there is some evidence that even in small quantities they can give primates diarrhoea.

Onions cause Heinz-body anaemia in all primates. Anaemia refers to a decrease in red blood cells. Given these are the cells that carry oxygen to tissue throughout the body this has significant consequences. The affected red blood cells will in fact burst. Depending on the degree of poisoning an affected marmoset will exhibit a range of symptoms. Even the tiny amounts of onion found in human baby food will be enough to make a Pygmy Marmoset ill.

Household *cockroaches* carry a parasite that causes serious illness in marmosets so they should never form part of the insect diet.

Chapter 8: Health management

Unfortunately Pygmy Marmosets are prone to a range of illnesses and health problems. What complicates this picture is the fact that humans and primates – including marmosets – can infect each other.

Like any other pet owner or animal caretaker, the 'parent' of a marmoset must become familiar with the normal behaviour of his or her pets. The reason why knowledge of "normal" is necessary is so one can very quickly spot changes in behaviour and appearance; these are often indicators of ill health or stress.

An owner also has a responsibility to familiarise him- or herself with the common diseases that these small primates are susceptible to and learn to recognise the signs and symptoms.

1) Early indications of health problems

These small primates are a bit like human children in that they can become very ill very quickly. It is therefore essential to monitor the behaviour and appearance of one's pets so one spots signs of trouble early on.

Primate vets also recommend that one takes a healthy marmoset's temperature daily for a week to use as a baseline. Then, if one suspects their pet may be ill one can take its temperature and have a healthy reading to compare it to.

General, early signs of ill-health in Pygmy Marmosets include:

- Hair loss
- Dull eyes
- Loss of interest in the world around it
- Lethargy
- Loss of appetite
- A limp, lifeless tail
- Erratic behaviour
- Atypical behaviour such as increased aggression
- Disturbed or poor sleep
- An increase of more than 2° in temperature

- Diarrhoea
- Vomiting.

If one's pet exhibits one or several of these it is time to consult a veterinarian who has experience with dealing with and treating primates.

2) *Choosing a vet*

You will most certainly need the services of a vet with experience treating primates including marmosets. These individuals and practises are not plentiful so it may be difficult to locate one.

Given this fact it is a good idea to ask the breeder you purchased your marmoset from for a recommendation or for contact details for a practise or primate care organisation in your area. Some owners have been assisted with referrals by local zoos or other primate owners. Joining online Pygmy Marmosets forums and interest groups is always a very good idea!

3) *Vaccinations*

Because of their similarities to human beings, and the fact that most of the illnesses they catch they pick up from people, primates are often given the same preventative vaccines that human children are given. The protection that the vaccines provide is for the sake of both the primate and the human care giver, as infections pass in both directions.

The vaccines given to various species of primates differ very significantly. For instance, gorillas and chimpanzees receive the full range of vaccines (flu, hepatitis, measles, polio, tetanus and sometimes rubella / German measles). Other primates such as lemurs are often only inoculated against rabies and only if they are at risk.

Pygmy Marmosets are a different case because of their size. It is felt by primate experts in both the US and the UK that one can use extremely low doses of vaccines but that this is dangerous. Their tiny stature makes these marmosets far more prone to experiencing serious adverse reactions to the vaccine.

Seeking the advice of a primate vet in the area is suggested, especially if it is a location where there is the danger of rabies.

4) The role of the vet: examinations, tests etc.

Many vets are not equipped in terms of resources or knowledge to deal with primates and in particular small, delicate ones such as Finger Monkeys. A vet must know how to restrain and hold a marmoset (without hurting it or being bitten) and how to diagnose and treat it effectively. Even taking blood or setting up a drip is a challenge with these small creatures. As a primate owner one is responsible for locating and getting to know a suitable vet.

Annual examination

There are several components of the annual examination a captive marmoset must have.

Firstly, he or she must be weighed to ensure that the animal is not over- or underweight. Dietary changes may be suggested if a marmoset is carrying too much weight. The reason why a primate is underweight must be investigated, as it may be a sign of an underlying medical issue.

A faecal sample must also be taken so that a culture can be performed. The aim is to look for a range of bacteria and viruses that are common in primates. A vet will often request culturing for Campylobacter, Salmonella, Shigella and Yersinia. In addition, this test looks for various types of internal parasites including various protozoa (single celled organisms) such as Giardia and worms.

In addition, a blood sample is drawn. A complete blood count (CBC) is done and this often reveals the presence of an infection and the strength of the immune system. It's also a fairly good indicator of overall health.

Vaccinations, as mentioned earlier, are not a standard feature of the medical care or preventative care of Pygmy Marmosets.

As part of the general physical examination the vet will look at the primate's teeth and gums to assess dental and periodontal health. If necessary the little patient will be sedated in order for the teeth to be cleaned.

Hospitalisation

A veterinary practice must also be familiar with the special care required by marmosets that are in their care due to injury, illness or following surgery.

Marmosets that are unwell, out of their usual environment and that are away from their usual companions need a number of conditions to be met for them to have a chance at recovery. These pint-sized patients need to be given additional warmth, handled as little as possible, kept in a darkened area to encourage sleep and kept well hydrated. Extra time and patience is needed to coax a sick marmoset to eat. For these reasons, ill finger monkeys are cared for at home whenever possible.

Because this species can become very ill extremely fast a vet may begin treatment before the test results are even back.

Necropsies

Due to the very real possibility of cross-infections or zoonosis between humans and marmosets, a necropsy (or animal autopsy) is always carried out when a primate dies in order to accurately determine the underlying illness.

It is essential that the cause of death is established so that medical authorities know whether the people in contact with the primate need to be tested and / or treated.

5) Health issues vets & owners watch for

An owner's first duty is to protect his or her pet and safeguard its health whenever possible. This includes protecting his or her pet from human-primate cross infections.

People suffering from a viral infection, including the Herpes strain (*Herpes simplex*) that causes cold sores, should not be allowed near marmosets as they may catch it. Even if a cold sore is not present the person is still a carrier of the virus and should not kiss or get too close to these vulnerable primates. Similarly, carriers of HIV or Hepatitis should not own primates because of the risk of cross-infection.

Furthermore, a viral infection like a cold sore that is painful and unsightly but not serious in people is rapidly fatal in infant and young marmosets; it causes a form of encephalitis.

Fortunately tuberculosis (TB) is extremely rare in marmosets so it is not a significant concern for owners or vets.

6) Protecting a marmoset from illness and injury

Three very important aspects of protecting the health of your marmoset(s) have been discussed: an annual vet examination, faecal cultures and not exposing the pet to anybody who is ill, especially with a viral infection. There are a couple of other things one can do:

- Always use a hand sanitiser before and after handling a primate, especially infants and babies as they are particularly vulnerable to infection.

- One shouldn't handle a pet marmoset too much. They are fragile little creatures and rough handling can result in injuries, even in broken bones. It is also extremely stressful for the pet.

  For this reason – among several others – a Pygmy Marmoset is not at all a suitable pet for very young children who have not learned how to handle animals yet.

- One must not let other people handle these pets. This applies to family, friends and strangers. Not only could they infect the marmoset but if frightened or stressed a pet primate may bite and infect the person who is bitten.

  If a pet primate bites someone, tests have to be carried out and, in some countries, there is a risk that the primate will be confiscated and even euthanized. The person who is bitten may also bring a legal case.

- One can't ignore signs of ill-health and one must be rigorous about watching for any changes in behaviour or appearance. If there is a suspicion that a Pygmy Marmoset is ill one must take it to a vet immediately.

Diarrhoea, for example, should not be ignored as it may indicate an infection, parasites or stress. One can't assume it's a temporary tummy upset. This condition can rapidly become serious, even fatal, in these tiny primates.

7) *Common diseases and ailments*

These diminutive primates are not hardy when they are in captivity. This is because they are exposed to bacteria and viruses carried by humans and can be infected easily. While they may fall victim to a range of problems some of the more serious and common are outlined here.

a) *Wasting Disease*

This is also known as "Wasting Syndrome" and "Marmoset Wasting Syndrome" due to its prevalence in this species.

Causes

This distressing and very serious illness is caused by a worm (*Trichospirura leptostoma*) that invades the pancreas. The carrier of this parasite is the domestic or household cockroach. This infestation of the pancreas causes it to malfunction. If a marmoset catches and eats an infected cockroach he or she ingests the eggs and will become ill.

Symptoms

Without a healthy pancreas, these primates become malnourished and dehydrated due to chronic diarrhoea. Despite the fact that an affected animal eats a great deal, it begins to lose body mass rapidly, hence the name of the condition.

In addition to becoming emaciated, these marmosets become lethargic and weak. Their coats become rough and hair loss around the tail is common. As the disease progresses the affected primate has problems with co-ordination and eventually suffers hindquarter paralysis. A large percentage of marmosets with this syndrome die.

Diagnosis

Marked weight loss combined with chronic diarrhoea are very good indicators of this disease. However, the diagnosis will be confirmed by a vet through a range of tests.

Blood tests will include a full blood count (CBC) and a blood chemistry profile. Low Calcium and protein levels and erratic white cell counts are all typical in blood from primates suffering from this syndrome.

Faecal tests to look for the presence of parasite eggs are performed. However, they are often not conclusive, as eggs are not shed constantly.

X-rays and ultrasound may also be used to look at the size and the general appearance of the pancreas.

Treatment and management

Most primates fare much better if they can be treated at home. A very ill animal will need hospitalisation, however. The patient must also be quarantined if he or she is likely to infect its companions. A vet is able to advise the owner in this regard.

Even before a definitive diagnosis of the specific parasite has been made, but there is diarrhoea and wasting, a vet will prescribe a broad spectrum medication such as fenbendazole as it will deal with a range of gastric parasites. This medication must be administered for 14 days. Parasites in the tissue of the pancreas are far harder to access and treat than in other organs.

A vet will also prescribe something to treat the diarrhoea. In addition, if there are secondary infections an antibiotic will be provided. Further intervention may include the use of vitamin and nutritional supplement products and pancreatic enzymes.

The medications can be administered by the owner by hiding it in or on a favourite sweet treat such as mashed banana or a piece of marshmallow.

Changes in diet are also necessary. Marmosets affected by wasting disease need a diet that is high in protein and easy to digest. Items such a scrambled eggs and cooked chicken are among the best options. Pets with this terrible disease must also be kept very well hydrated.

Unwell primates need a little extra tender loving care. For instance, a marmoset with chronic diarrhoea and marked weight loss feels the cold even more than usual. The use of a heating pad set on a low heat and covered with a towel will make him or her feel more comfortable.

Prevention

There are several things an owner can do to protect against this parasite and the potentially life-threatening condition it causes:

- Never feed cockroaches to marmosets

- Have a pet dewormed from time to time. A primate vet will be able to suggest the best schedule so that there is protection but so that deworming is not done needlessly or too often.

- Keeping the enclosure or cage and surrounding area or building clean so that cockroaches don't breed is very important. If the insects wander into an area where primates are they will be eaten!

Finally, one must watch any primate that has recovered from the syndrome very carefully. The reason for this is that relapses are possible (and in some individuals they are more likely) and they must be dealt with both immediately and aggressively in order to save the animal's life.

b) Bacterial infections

Causes

There are a large number of bacteria that cause infections and illnesses in primates, including in Pygmy Marmosets.

Infections can be acquired through ingesting contaminated food; being bitten by an infected animal; coming into contact with a sick primate or other animal including squirrels, weasels, rodents, and human beings.

Symptoms

The nature, range and severity of the symptoms depend on what bacterium is involved and which organ(s) and body system(s) have been affected.

For instance, *Yersinia pseudotuberculosis* is a gram-negative bacterium caused by contaminated food. Symptoms are similar to tuberculosis (TB) and may also cause severe tissue damage in the liver, spleen and the lymph nodes.

To complicate matters it is also possible for a primate to contract more than one bacterial infection at the same time.

Diagnosis and treatment

The method of diagnosis and course of treatment depend on the nature and the bacteria and the severity of the infection.

A thorough physical examination and the taking of a medical history are standard elements of a vet consultation for a sick animal. Blood and faecal tests are usually involved and other diagnostic measures such as X-rays and scans may also be employed.

Prevention

Bacterial infections generally are less likely to occur if one provides wholesome food, fresh water, a safe environment where pets are not exposed to sick animals or people and if one maintains high levels of cleanliness and hygiene.

A vet can advise about preventative measures for specific infections.

c) Herpes Simplex

Herpes simplex is one of the biggest killers of marmosets in captivity. It is their proximity to humans that places them at risk of this painful and invariably fatal condition.

Cause

An estimated 80% of people carry the Herpes Simplex 1 virus and the majority of them will never exhibit symptoms or even know they are infected. The virus is dormant for much of the time and lives in the largest nerve in the face (the trigeminal nerve, broadly speaking, impacts on the eye, lips and upper and lower jaws making chewing and facial movement possible).

In humans, the symptom – cold sores or fever blisters – only appears when the carrier is ill or stressed. The virus is transmitted through saliva during this active or symptomatic period. However, because marmosets are so highly susceptible, carriers can transmit the virus to them even when there are no symptoms at all.

Symptoms

A marmoset infected with Herpes Simplex will be lethargic, have no appetite, be running a high fever and will have diarrhoea.

As the disease worsens sores / lesions and or blisters develop on the tongue, inner cheeks and the gums, the lips swell, there may be evidence of some facial paralysis (visible drooping and an inability to blink) and, later, seizures.

Diagnosis

Diagnosis is often made on the basis of a physical examination only as laboratory test results for the virus may not be received before the virus has run its fatal course.

Treatment

There is no cure for this virus and, like all viruses, it doesn't respond at all to antibiotics. Treatment is therefore supportive. In other words, the vet will do all he or she can to treat the symptoms and the pain.

Given the severity of the pain and the fact that an infected marmoset will die, most vets recommend euthanasia as the kind and loving course of action.

Prevention

Anyone who has a cold sore must not be allowed to go near a marmoset. These tiny primates can catch the virus from the saliva of a carrier who has no symptoms or from someone who is a carrier and doesn't know it because they've never had symptoms.

It is therefore essential that the owners of these primates never:

- Kiss their marmosets on the mouth
- Allow the pet to kiss them on the mouth or near the mouth
- Let the marmoset eat from a person's mouth
- Feed a pet anything that has been in a human's mouth or may have saliva on it
- Give it anything to play with that may have saliva on it.

This virus is mild in humans but the danger it represents to Pygmy Marmosets can't be underestimated.

d) Lymphocytic Choriomeningitis

Lymphocytic Choriomeningitis or LCMV is a viral illness that captive marmosets may contract.

Cause

This virus is carried and spread by mice and is present in their urine, saliva and faeces. It is possible that a mouse may take up residence in a marmoset enclosure. However, it is enough if it just moves through the cage and leaves infected matter behind that captive marmosets then come into contact with it.

Symptoms

An infected Finger Monkey will lose its appetite and become very lethargic, short of breath as the lungs are affected and jaundiced. The jaundice results in a yellowing of the eyes and the skin. There may also be bleeding under the skin and in muscle tissue. This viral infection is usually fatal in Pygmy Marmosets.

Diagnosis

The vet will perform a thorough physical examination, obtain a medical history from the owner and take blood to test for the specific antibody associated with the virus and to assess liver function. For further confirmation, a vet may also take X-rays and do a scan. However, this is unlikely, as the tests will cause further stress and pain to an already very ill little creature.

Treatment

The disease can't be cured in these primates so treatment is supportive; symptoms are managed as they develop and everything is done to make the sick animal as comfortable as possible. Vets may well recommend euthanasia as the humane option.

Prevention

It's important to guard against the possibility of mice getting into a primate enclosure. Various options are available to ensure this. Indoor cages are less at risk in a home with good levels of general hygiene and no pet mice that are allowed to wander around.

The good news is that this virus is fairly easy to deal with as it is destroyed by most disinfectants and detergents. It is also inactivated by ultraviolet light which one uses for marmosets in any event to provide the necessary D3.

e) Parasite infestations

There are a range of nasty parasites that marmosets may become host to in addition to the *Trichospirura leptostoma* or pancreas worm discussed earlier:

- *Giardia*: the symptoms are chronic diarrhoea and, as a result, inadequate absorption of nutrients.
- *Prosthenorchis elegans* / thorny-headed worm is carried by cockroaches and lives in the intestine of the host.
- *Enterobius vermicularis* / human pinworm: a severe infestation causes serious enteritis which can be fatal.
- *Baylisascaris procyonis*: this is a species of roundworm that can infest the cerebrospinal fluid with very serious consequences.
- *Gongylonema pulchrum* / gullet worm: these live in the blood vessels of the mouth and throat.

Diagnosis

A full physical examination will be done and a medical history taken. Faecal tests to look for the presence of parasite eggs will be carried out in an effort to identify the type of parasite involved. However, they may not be conclusive, as eggs are not shed constantly by all species of parasites. X-rays and ultrasound may also be used to look at the size and the general appearance of the major organs.

Treatment

With many parasites it is unlikely that the primate will require hospitalisation. However, this depends on the nature of the parasite, the severity of the infestation and whether or not secondary health problems have developed.

The vet will prescribe a broad spectrum medication such as fenbendazole which deals with a range of internal parasites. This medication must be administered for 14 days.

With thorny-headed worms surgery is needed, as they can't be removed through the use of medication.

A vet will prescribe an antibiotic to treat secondary infections and an anti-diarrhoeal if that is necessary. Further intervention may include the use of vitamin and nutritional supplement products.

Prevention

There are several things an owner can do to protect against parasites.

Firstly, don't ever feed cockroaches to marmosets. Secondly, have pet primates dewormed periodically. A primate vet will suggest the best schedule so that there is protection but deworming is not done unnecessarily or too often. Finally, keep the enclosure and surrounding area or building clean.

f) Metabolic Bone Disease

Metabolic Bone Disease (MBD) can occur in both young and adult Pygmy Marmosets in captivity although it is more common in juvenile animals that are still growing.

It's also known by a myriad other names including nutritional secondary hyperparathyroidism, rickets, osteoporosis, osteogenesis imperfecta, cage paralysis, bone atrophy, juvenile osteoporosis, paper-bone disease and Paget's disease.

Causes

This condition is caused by a vitamin and mineral deficiency or imbalance. This applies specifically to calcium, vitamin D and phosphorous, all of which are essential for marmosets. If a pet suffers from this disease the responsibility lies squarely with the owner.

Babies that are weaned too young, captive marmosets that are fed an inadequate diet or primates that have no exposure to natural sunlight or ultraviolet light are at risk of developing this condition. Infants born to mothers who have the condition are also high risk individuals.

Symptoms

As the name implies, the animal's bones are affected by this condition.

Limbs become bent and distorted, the tail may develop angled bends, the spine and ribs may be deformed and misshapen. In severe cases where the ribs are badly affected, the abdominal organs may begin to protrude. The pelvis may collapse resulting in extreme constipation or even bowel obstruction. The jaw is often affected – it becomes swollen and slack – which makes chewing very difficult.

In very young animals the teeth may emerge crooked or not at all because of jaw deformities. The compromised bones are also prone to break and fracture easily.

As the illness worsens, twitches and tremors develop. With time, these turn into either seizures (convulsions) or muscle rigidity. Paralysis may occur with some animals.

Diagnosis

X-rays are carried out of the entire animal so that the shape of bones, including the spine and pelvis, and any fractures can be identified.

Blood tests are also done to measure calcium and phosphorous levels although they don't always provide definitive results. A more helpful test looks at serum alkaline phosphate levels.

The importance of a thorough physical examination can't be underestimated. The owner and vet must handle the marmoset with great care and gentleness because of the brittleness of the bones; fractures occur very easily.

Treatment

A popular and common treatment is a course of calcium supplements that can be given in oral or injectable form. This is followed by weekly injections of a drug marketed as Calcitonin-salmon or Calcimar. Treatment is stopped when the marmoset is able to move and walk normally.

Animals that have been untreated for prolonged periods and have suffered marked deformation of bones as a result will never recover. However, their general well-being will benefit from treatment as it will stop some of the symptoms.

Prevention

This condition can be prevented by ensuring that babies are not weaned too young and that all captive Pygmy Marmosets receive the correct nutrition, exposure or natural or ultraviolent light and adequate nutritional supplements when environmental conditions are not optimal.

g) Urinary tract diseases

Although infections of the bladder (called bacterial cystitis) and kidneys are not common in marmosets generally they do sometimes happen. They are also more common in females than in males.

Causes

The usual cause of these infections is bacteria, which enter the opening of the urethra on the outside and then travel up to the bladder where they set up an infection. Far less usual is a bacterial infection of the blood affecting the bladder.

Kidney infections are almost invariably the result of untreated and / or severe bladder infections. The bacteria travel from the bladder further up the urethra to the kidneys. A kidney infection is far more concerning as the primate suffers from more severe symptoms and, if kidney function becomes compromised, there can be multiple complications.

Symptoms

The infection causes spasms, which in turn lead to the urge to urinate and to more frequent urination. Affected animals often strain as they feel the need to urinate but are unable to do so.

Given the animal urinates far more often, only a small amount is produced each time. The urine itself may have a stronger odour than usual and may be pink or streaked with red due to the presence of blood or small blood clots.

Urination often results in pain and a burning sensation. As a result, primates may rub their genitalia on surfaces or with their hands in an effort to ease the pain. Swelling of the female's genitals may be visible.

The symptoms of a kidney infection are the same as for a bladder infection but these little patients will also have a fever and will probably be lethargic, sleep more than usual and may even go off their food. With a kidney problem, toxins begin to enter the bloodstream and, if left untreated, the kidneys suffer damage, which will lead to serious consequences for the body as a whole.

Diagnosis

A physical examination is performed and a medical history obtained from the owner.

The only test that is usually performed is a urine test. These tests look for the presence red and white blood cells, pus, bacteria, nitrites, glucose, urinary tract cells and crystals. Crystals indicate bladder stones which, fortunately, are very rare in primates generally.

The vet must be provided with a sample that is as fresh as possible and one that is taken from the substrate or floor of a cage or enclosure is not helpful in terms of testing for bacteria. The urine should be placed in a clean, dry container so there is no contamination that may confuse the test result.

If necessary, the vet will take a urine sample by using a catheter, expressing urine by using gentle pressure on the bladder or by drawing urine out of the bladder with a needle. All three methods are carried out while the marmoset is sedated.

Treatment

A specific antibiotic is prescribed if a bacterial culture could be done. If not, the vet will prescribe a broad spectrum antibiotic to deal with the infection.

It is important to ensure that the marmoset has access to fresh, clean water and the usual balanced diet.

Prevention

It is not easy to protect primates from bacteria. However, maintaining good hygiene in the enclosure will go a long way to reduce the chances of this already uncommon ailment.

h) Cardiac disease

While cardiac or heart disease is not uncommon in many larger primates and Old World Monkeys, it isn't often encountered in Pygmy Marmosets.

Causes

There are a range of conditions which could affect the heart. However, the most likely one to be encountered is hypertension or high blood pressure. The marmosets that are most at risk are ones that are overweight.

Symptoms

The nature, range and severity of the symptoms depend on the nature and extent of the cardiac or cardio-vascular condition. With more severe conditions symptoms may include lethargy and breathlessness.

Diagnosis and treatment

The method of diagnosis and course of treatment depend on the nature and severity of the condition.

A thorough physical examination and the taking of a medical history are standard elements of a vet consultation. Blood tests and other diagnostic measures such as X-rays and scans may also be employed.

Prevention

It's vital to provide a balanced, healthy diet and the right dietary supplements. While one can give a pet treats, it is essential not to overdo it and to monitor a marmoset's weight.

Being overweight, stressed and not having enough space in which to be active increase the risk of cardiac and vascular conditions. An annual vet check-up will monitor weight and blood pressure.

i) Coprophagy

Coprophagy refers to the eating of faeces and this behaviour occurs in many species including domestic dogs and some primates. It is, however, rare in all species of marmosets.

Causes

Contrary to popular belief, marmosets that engage in coprophagy are not doing so because they are either bored or hungry. This behaviour is thought to be linked to a lack of protein or other deficiencies in their diet.

Diagnosis

Diagnosis is easy as it is based on observation of behaviour.

Treatment

Treatment is unnecessary unless the animal has contracted a bacterial infection as a result of eating faecal matter. The vet will identify the specific bacteria and prescribe a course of antibiotics.

Prevention

If a captive Pygmy Marmoset is being fed a healthy, fully nutritional diet and is given the correct quantities and variety of foods it is extremely unlikely that it will develop this behaviour.

j) Tail alopecia

Marmosets may develop alopecia (hair loss or bald spots). The most common area is at the base of the tail.

Causes

There are various possible causes for this condition. They include over-grooming (self grooming or by other group members), excessive scent marking, skin conditions or – and this is the most serious possibility – an infestation of pancreatic worms.

Diagnosis

Diagnosis will be based initially on a thorough physical examination and taking a medical history. If an owner has not noticed excessive grooming or marking behaviour and there is no evidence of a skin condition or reaction, then underlying conditions must be looked for.

Treatment

Treatment will be based on the cause and established diagnosis.

Prevention

If the cause is behavioural a vet or primate specialist may be able to offer advice as to how to stop the problem behaviour. If it is medical the vet will prescribe medication and or dietary changes.

k) Nappy or diaper rash

Clearly this condition is only a possibility in marmosets that wear nappies! This rash is a form of dermatitis that is uncomfortable but not serious unless it is neglected and an infection develops.

Causes

If a nappy, especially a soiled one, is left on too long a moist, warm environment is created which leads to irritation of the skin.

The acidity in urine and the dampness created by faeces can also cause this type of dermatitis. Faecal matter contains bacteria and can lead to secondary infections when it comes in contact with skin that is inflamed or broken.

Symptoms

The affected skin looks red and shiny. In severe cases, it may even have a raw appearance and bleed slightly. The genitals may also become inflamed. If there is pus this is an indication of infection.

Diagnosis

Nothing other than a physical examination and taking a medical history is necessary to diagnose this ailment. However, if there is a bad infection, swabs or samples on the infected matter may be taken in order to identify the bacterium involved.

Treatment

A topical ointment will be recommended. These preparations form a protective layer over the skin so moisture can't get through. It should be noted that many of these products contain Zinc Oxide. The toxicity is low but if a primate ingests a significant amount over time it can be harmful.

If an infection is present treatment will consist of an antibiotic.

Ointments and creams are not easy to use on little bottoms that are covered in hair! It is therefore far better to prevent this rash than have to deal with it.

Prevention

There are a number of steps the owner of a Pygmy Marmoset can take to prevent or at least significantly reduce the risk of this type of dermatitis:

- ✓ Don't use a nappy unless it is essential
- ✓ Change the nappy as soon as it has been soiled
- ✓ Don't put a nappy on too tightly so that some air can penetrate the fabric
- ✓ If using cloth nappies they must be washed in a mild detergent and rinsed very thoroughly. Bleach and fabric softeners should not be used.
- ✓ Disposable nappies are preferable to cloth ones as they are more absorbent and often have a barrier fabric that keeps the moisture from the primate's fur and skin
- ✓ Avoid using baby wipes as they can contain alcohol which can dry out or even burn the skin

l) Flies

Flies are especially an issue with outdoor enclosures. When present these insects can cause some health problems and at best they will annoy, irritate and distress your marmosets.

The bites from more aggressive, larger flies such as horseflies could leave raised bumps some of which may even bleed slightly. While flies will be an unavoidable part of a pet's life, one can help to deter them or at least reduce the numbers:

- Remove faecal matter regularly
- Keeping the cage or enclosure clean
- Keep feed and water bowls clean
- Use fly traps or strips near but outside the cage or enclosure. Do *not* place them where the marmosets can reach them, as they are toxic.

While some owners use herbal or plant-based repellents there is not a great deal of scientific evidence to prove that they do work.

m) Ticks and fleas

Ticks and fleas are parasites that feed on the host's blood. There are some tick species that are found all over the world and others that are specific to certain continents and locations.

Ticks are more prevalent in some areas such as those where there is long grass or untreated livestock. These insects are also more of a problem in spring and summer than during colder times of the year.

It can be fairly easy to spot ticks. One will also feel them when cuddling a pet. Ticks engorged with blood are especially hard to miss as they become large and bloated.

Different tick species are different sizes and colours. They are often found on where the blood supply is close to the surface and the tick is protected and harder to rub off such as the ears, under the tail and between the back legs.

Treatment and prevention

Removing a tick that has gorged itself on blood is not a pleasant experience for the marmoset or owner. It's also not easy to remove some ticks. If they are not removed at all or completely they don't just cause irritation to a pet; they may also pose risk of greater infection.

Older methods of removing a tick including smothering it in something oily or greasy (like Vaseline) or burning them should *not* be used as they usually cause the dying tick to regurgitate which forces toxins into the host's bloodstream.

Ideally you want to keep ticks away or prevent them rather than dealing with them once they have latched onto your pet. However options are limited.

There are anti-tick shampoos designed for cats and dogs that kill ticks on contact. But it is vital that you check with a primate vet first before using any product to make sure it is safe and will do the job. A vet or local primate centre will be able to suggest better or other options.

Removing ticks and keeping them away is one part of the war against these nasty parasites. One also needs to treat the environment. Again, speak to an expert for advice on products that are sprinkled or sprayed on the ground, bedding and other areas your pet uses. One must ensure that the product will not be harmful or toxic if ingested or on contact.

There are a large number of different ticks. Some tick bites will also cause local irritation. Others are potentially far more serious. While some carry the same diseases, other illnesses are specific to one species of tick. What's more, certain tick species carry more than one disease. Tick-borne diseases can be hard to spot. There are several common diseases that affect both primates and, often, humans.

- Lyme disease: This infection leads to lameness. In worst case scenarios, or severe cases, this illness is fatal. Diagnosis is difficult as many of the symptoms mimic other illnesses.

Symptoms may be slow to emerge and can come and go. The primary symptoms are short-term lameness that lasts several days, fatigue and lethargy and loss of appetite.

- Tick paralysis: This is not so much a disease as a very severe reaction to the toxin that ticks secrete. This toxin attacks the central nervous system.

  Symptoms include loss of appetite, nausea, inability to regulate body temperature, weakness, lethargy and partial or full paralysis. More severe symptoms are difficulty swallowing and then with breathing. Death usually follows.

8) Zoonotic illnesses

A zoonotic disease is one which both humans and other animals can get and which they can give to, and catch from, each other.

So, while an owner and any other people in contact with a primate may become ill, people pose the same risk to primates. However, a Pygmy Marmoset is more likely to be infected than to infect. In addition to *Herpes Simplex*, humans have been known to infect marmosets with influenza, tuberculosis and rubella (measles).

One can reduce the risk of infection – in either direction – through good hygiene practises including thorough hand washing and taking protective steps such as wearing gloves when cleaning and handling excrement. If a primate carer has a cold, flu or a cold sore then he or she should not enter the primate enclosure or handle the animals at all.

Understandably, certain zoonotic illnesses cause more concern among health care individuals and bodies and primate owners than others.

Potential human to primate infections

- *Herpes simplex*: see page 63 for a discussion of this highly infectious virus which is invariably fatal for marmosets.

- *Tuberculosis*: the bacteria that causes this serious respiratory illness are spread in the saliva which can become airborne. A person with TB that coughs on or near a primate may infect it. A sick primate can also infect humans and other primates.

This illness is extremely serious and usually fatal in primates. While TB is usually associated with the respiratory system / the lungs, it is in fact a systemic illness as it may infect and affect any number or organs.

The good news is that New World monkeys like Pygmy Marmosets are less likely to contract this infection than other primates. The bad news is that often sick animals show no symptoms until they are very ill indeed. If there are symptoms they can include coughing, weakness, loss of appetite, weight loss, lethargy and a dull coat. If the TB attacks the brain, seizures occur. Spinal TB results in paralysis and if the bacteria invade the intestine it causes severe diarrhoea.

Treatment involves the use of multiple drugs and remedies to deal with the symptoms such as diarrhoea. However, some primates die before symptoms appear and in many cases euthanasia may be the best option.

- *Measles*: like TB this infection spreads very easily from humans to primates and is also an airborne pathogen. Measles in human children and adults can cause serious complications but the illness is fatal for marmosets.

  The measles virus attacks the lymphatic, gastrointestinal and respiratory systems in marmosets and does severe damage to all the affected organs.

  The vaccine for this illness is very effective but is not always administered to these little primates because of the size. An infected animal will die and so, in all probability, it would be kinder to euthanize.

Potential primate to human infections

- *Serious viral illnesses*: in theory, wild-caught as opposed to captive bred primates may be carriers of deadly viruses such as a number of the haemorrhagic fevers like Ebola. The possibility is small but it makes a compelling case for only obtaining a pet from a breeder and not from the wild!

- *Enteric / intestinal viruses or bacteria*: these pathogens are transmitted in faecal matter. If that is transferred somehow onto or into the mouth infection will occur. To avoid this, one must use protective equipment such as gloves and ensure proper hygiene in terms of affected surfaces and hand washing.

- *Salmonellosis*: *salmonella* bacteria are also found in primate faeces and causes serious gastric illness in humans: cramps, fever and diarrhoea. Untreated, this infection can spread to the bloodstream leading to serious complications.

- *Shigellosis*: this as another bacterium that is carried and transmitted in faeces. The symptoms in humans are the same as those for *salmonella* except that the diarrhoea is usually bloody. The infection usually clears on its own after about 5 days.

- *Giardiasis*: this condition is the result of ingesting the *Giardia* parasite. Symptoms include stomach cramps, nausea and diarrhoea, which last for 2 to 6 weeks. Treatment must be obtained from a doctor in order to deal with an infestation.

- *Cryptosporidium*: this is a parasite found in many mammals and not only primates. The eggs are shed in the faecal matter of host animals. The bad news is that this parasite is moderately resistant to most disinfectants. In humans, the parasite causes diarrhoea which will stop on its own after a week or two. However, elderly people or those with weak immune systems may become seriously ill.

Protecting both humans and marmosets from infection

There are a number of things one can do to prevent infection:

- ✓ *Thorough hand washing*: this is without a doubt one of the most important protective and preventative measures one can implement. Use soap and warm water and carefully lather and rinse each finger, the thumbs, between fingers and the palms and backs of the hands. Children must be assisted or taught to wash their hands properly after playing with a pet primate. Many breeders also recommend using a hand sanitiser before and after handling a primate, particularly a young or ill animal.

✓ *Use protective gear*: when cleaning and sanitising a cage or enclosure, or changing a primate's nappy, it is advisable to wear gloves. If one is working with cage substrate that contains faecal matter or wiping down surfaces that may be contaminated it is suggested that one also wears a face mask.

Potential danger posed by bites and scratches

There is the possibility that pathogens may be present in the mouth, saliva or under the nails of primates. These can be transferred through puncture wounds from teeth or through scratches that break the skin.

If one gets bitten or scratched one must wash the injury site very thoroughly with soap and water. It should also be monitored for signs of inflammation or infection. If one develops other symptoms it is important to seek medical advice and tell the practitioner about the incident.

9) How to give a marmoset medication

Even pets such as dogs that are domesticated and co-operative can be difficult to give medication to. Administering a pill – an antibiotic, de-wormer or a supplement – can be very stressful for the pet and the owner. Antibiotics in particular can be extremely bitter and given these primates are so tiny the pills have to be cut up. This releases all the bitterness, which also leaves a very nasty after-taste.

Pygmy Marmosets are very smart and have excellent memories. He or she may fall for the bitter-pill-hidden-in-something-sweet trick once but they won't make the same mistake twice! The owner has to use all his or her ingenuity to medicate their primate.

It also helps if the vet can prescribe a less awful tasting tablet or a liquid or a paediatric suspension. Some of these children's medications taste very nice and primates drink it with enthusiasm.

Others are also a little nasty-tasting but they can be mixed with something like a bit of fruit juice.

Marmosets are also reluctant to take medications that have little or no taste. For example, the pastes often used to treat parasites (including the serious pancreatic worm) are chalky that primates don't enjoy. However, because there's so little innate flavour it can be more successfully hidden in or on a favourite sweet treat.

One specialist primate vet came up with an ingenious way of treating sick marmosets that didn't cause the little patients additional stress. A liquid medication dose was injected into several mealworms which were then fed to the ill marmoset. For those owners who don't feel up to this it could be injected into pieces of fruit or mixed into fruit juice.

One should talk to the vet and be creative. What one must avoid is forcing medication down a pet's throat, trick a pet or give up and stop administering the medication.

10) A First Aid Kit

While one can't prepare for every eventuality, it is a good idea to keep a first aid kit on hand so you can treat your little marmoset immediately if the need arises. The basic kit, kept in a clearly marked, clean and air-tight container should include the following items:

- Disposable gloves (2 pairs)
- Gauze squares (various sizes)
- Gauze swabs (various sizes)
- First aid tape
- Rolls of gauze bandage
- Rolls of self-adhering bandage (sometimes called "vet wrap")
- Round-end scissors
- Tweezers
- Small torch
- Magnifying glass
- Rectal thermometer (ensure it is a suitable size for a Pygmy Marmoset!)

- Lubricant
- Hand sanitiser.

It's a good idea to also have a few medications in the kit. It is essential, though, to be guided by a breeder or your vet as to which ones will be safe for your pet. Basics could include:

- Mild antiseptic / cleansing solution
- Mild antiseptic cream
- Vitamin solution
- A vet may suggest a broad spectrum antibiotic for certain animals.

Include details of the dates of vaccinations, deworming treatments and tetanus shots in case the vet needs this information or you are not there to provide it.

In an emergency one is not always thinking clearly so having the numbers you need to hand can save precious time. Have a card or list that includes your vet's number (including an after hours or emergency number), a local marmoset sanctuary, the poison helpline and any other local resources that would be useful.

11) Microchipping

The reason to have a micro-chip inserted is to help to trace your pet Pygmy Marmoset if it gets lost or stolen. After all these intelligent, agile creatures are impressive escape artists and desirable too.

Although a chip can be effective, it is not fool-proof. The down side is that having a chip will only help if someone finds your pet and takes him or her to a shelter. Also, while most animal shelters have scanners and use them, this is not true of all of them. This is why also having a collar and tag is a good idea.

The procedure for inserting a chip is fairly simple and should be done by a vet. A large needle is used to place the chip, which is about the size of a grain of rice, under the skin, usually between the shoulder blades. A special scanner can read the unique number on the chip.

The procedure only takes a few seconds and the sensation is the same as having blood drawn. In other words, there is a little pain and discomfort but it is very brief. There is an extremely small possibility of complications happening after the chip implant. For instance, a few domestic animals such as cats have developed tumours at the site where the chip was placed. This is, however, statistically very unlikely.

The chips used in different parts of the world also utilize different frequencies. The UK and Europe use a 134.2 kilohertz chip while a 125 and 128 kilohertz chip is used in America.

If one is going to transport a pet across a border one should check on the requirements as some countries have regulations about both chip date and type. Permits will in all probability be required too!

At time of writing the cost of micro-chipping was in the region of $50 in the US and up to about £40 in the UK depending on when it's done and who does it.

12) Primate medical aid

Having a sick Pygmy Marmoset is stressful and upsetting. It can also be very costly and these kinds of expenses are difficult to budget for.

If you give your Finger Monkey the right diet and environment, arrange annual check-ups at the vet and protect your pet from people who are infectious it should stay pretty healthy. Of course, no animal is completely safe from illness and even the healthiest one can be injured.

Enter pet insurance. Depending on where you are you may be able to opt to take out one of several types of cover to help you with bills when your pint-sized primate needs medical care. Some insurers offer the choice of a plan that covers expenses in the event of an accident only. Others will pay costs for both accident and illness. The third option, one that usually gets added onto one of the others, is to cover standard procedures and costs such as dental cleaning and routine check-ups.

Like most insurance, these policies will have a deductible or excess that you will have to pay, but they can help greatly if your marmoset ever requires significant or ongoing treatment or vet care. The premium and affordability will also vary depending on the type of cover chosen and how many pets you place on the policy.

Your vet should be able to supply you with a brochure, pamphlet or information. You will have to weigh the cost of insurance against the possibility of being out of pocket at a later date.

Chapter 9: Pygmy Marmoset reproduction

Those fortunate enough to have marmosets may be tempted to breed with them. The advice from the majority of primate specialists is: "Don't!" Unless one has solid experience with primate care in general and Pygmy Marmoset husbandry in particular, one should *not* breed these tiny monkeys.

There are also a number of legalities one has to comply with in the US. Firstly, one must have a USDA license, which is regulated by the Department of Agriculture's Animal and Plant Health Inspection Service. In addition one requires a license from the state and often permission from the city or county. Failure to comply results in harsh fines. As it should be, all of this legislation is there to protect the primates, not the breeders. American breeders are subject to inspections, which must be passed in order to retain the license.

There are far too many pet marmosets and a high proportion of them find themselves unwanted when the cuteness factor has worn off or the owner discovers how much work they are.

One can get contraceptives from a vet in order to prevent unwanted pregnancy in pet marmosets. This issue must be taken seriously because a female marmoset can produce babies every 5 to 6 months from the time she is 15 months old. There is also no mating season so pregnancies occur year round. Each pregnancy leads to the birth of twins or – although rare – triplets or even quadruplets.

It should also be kept in mind that hand rearing these pint-sized, delicate primates is a difficult and extremely demanding task! If infants are weaned too young they may suffer long-term from medical problems because they didn't receive the antibodies and colostrum found in mother's milk.

In addition to the nutrition infants receive from their mothers they also receive a great deal of emotional care from their father and the rest of the troop. This, too, must be provided by a human carer in the absence of a parent or primate carer.

Young may nurse for up to three months and infants are carried on the back of a parent or other troop member. They also seek out their parents when they are frightened or startled and only reach maturity after 3 to 6 months.

1) Reproduction and rearing in the wild

Pygmy Marmosets are usually monogamous. The breeding pair stays together and will produce several generations of young.

As previously indicated there is no specific mating season for these primates. However, in the wild there are two requirements that must be met before Pygmy Marmosets will mate and produce offspring. Firstly, they must have secure shelter and, secondly, there must be an adequate supply of food.

If those conditions are met then the female will produce twins. (In captivity where there is stable shelter and no shortage of food it is not unusual for mothers to give birth to three or even four infants after each mating.) The gestation period is $4^1/_2$ months on average.

These thumb-sized babies weigh about 0.4 – 0.5 ounces or 3 – 15 grams. They are far more demanding and fragile than other primate infants and they need constant attention. Because of their size they can only eat very small amounts. However, they get hungry every couple of hours.

In the wild only an estimated 25% of babies survive and reach maturity. Others are taken by predators, become ill, fall out of nests or trees or even get lost after falling off the adult they were riding on. A further cause of infant mortality is that mothers of multiple infants may not be able to produce enough milk for all of them.

It is not only the mother that is an active caregiver. The father acts as midwife and helps to deliver the babies. He then cleans them and assumes the full-time care role. The father carries the infant(s) on his back for the first couple of weeks. They are only brought to their mother so they can nurse. Dad might get some time off if older siblings babysit for a while!

The act of caring for infants teaches older, juvenile siblings the parenting skills they will need later on. Females may even delay having offspring of their own until younger siblings are more independent. Some studies have shown that juvenile females are in fact able to 'switch off' ovulation until they are ready to mate and produce their own young.

Very new infants do not travel with the troop when it goes foraging. They are left hidden in the nest until the group returns. Only when they are old and strong enough to cling to an adult as it climbs and leaps will they travel with the group.

By the time the babies are weaned (at about 3 months) they are able to accompany the group on foraging trips. When they reach the age of 2 years they may leave to start their own family or group or stay on to look after the next generation.

2) Developmental stages

A system where childcare is provided by various members of the social group is known as co-operative care. With Pygmy Marmosets this takes several forms. The activities of the parents and older siblings in terms of carrying and caring for infants and un-weaned babies have already been discussed.

In addition to this, group members are involved in disciplining the young, sharing food with them when they begin to eat solids and teaching them how to forage and raise young. In other words, the care and education of the young is undertaken by the group as a whole.

In terms of development there are certain behaviours, activities and milestones at various stages or up to specific ages:

> *Birth to 3 weeks*: infants are carried 'piggy-back' style on the back of an adult at all times. The only exception is when the babies are nursing.

> While the adults are able to climb and even run with a baby on their backs, they take turns so babies are transferred from one adult to another.

> It is during this very early stage in development that Pygmy Marmosets begin to interact at a social level with their parents,

siblings and the other group members. These bonds are crucial, especially in the wild.

➤ *From 4 weeks*: at this stage the baby marmoset is getting strong enough not to need to be carried all the time. Like the young of many species it may need to be encouraged to stand on its own feet.

Its family members may 'help' the process along by giving the baby tiny nips and gentle shoves to get it off an adult's back. Young raised in captivity may feel secure enough to leave the adult's back earlier than they do in the wild where there are far more dangers and threats.

➤ *The exploration phase:* once the youngster has been persuaded to leave the backs of the adults he or she will begin to explore the environment. As with other young this involves touching, sniffing and tasting objects to determine what they are.

Young at this stage that are in captivity need to be provided with additional stimulation. This can take the form of toys, new objects of various textures and shapes that are introduced to the enclosure or just moving items from time to time. This stimulation is essential for their intellectual development.

As they gain strength and confidence the young spend less and less time being carried by an adult. If a baby becomes startled it will run to an adult to be comforted. The adult marmosets are constantly on the look-out for danger. If there is a threat the adult nearest to the baby will pick it up and run with it.

➤ *After 8 weeks:* at this stage youngsters are only carried in unusual circumstances; this happens very occasionally.

Babies in captivity may be weaned at about 6 weeks. However, their wild counter-parts are only weaned after 8 to 10 weeks when they have absorbed all the nutrients and antibodies they require from mother's milk. The components in the milk ensure that the babies grow normally, have built strong bones and developed a robust immune system.

3) Growth milestones

- *At birth*:
  - The eyes are open or will open within the first three days after birth
  - The tufts of hair in the ears have not appeared yet
  - Weight is about 30 grams or 1 ounce
  - The length (head and body) is approximately 6 – 8 centimetres or 2 – 3 inches
  - The body hair is grey and very fine in texture
  - There is less hair on the chest and tummy so that the infant can more easily absorb the body heat of the adult that is carrying it
  - The tail is also grey in colour but it has slightly darker grey bands

- *Second week*:
  - The infant is able to crawl
  - The adults carry it at all times unless it is nursing

- *Third week*:
  - Still nursing but begins to accept solid foods
  - Continues to be carried by adults

- *Fourth week*:
  - The baby begins to leave the adult caretaker occasionally in order to explore its surroundings
  - Still nursing and spending most of its time on an adult's back
  - The infant spontaneously urinates and defecates without the need for stimulation by an adult

- *Fifth week*:
  - The baby continues to explore its surroundings
  - Still nursing and sleeping a lot but is spending less time on an adult's back
  - The baby begins to lap liquids

- *Sixth week*:
  - Weight should now be approximately 70 grams or 2.5 ounces

- The baby's full set of milk teeth have come through by this stage
- The baby can now be weaned if necessary and fed a combination of milk substitutes and solid foods
- It begins to try new foods

- *Seventh week*:
    - The baby's weight should now reach 80 grams or 2.8 ounces

- *Eighth week*:
    - The length of the head and body has increased to 14 – 17 centimetres or 5 – 6 inches
    - The baby's weight has now increased to 91 grams or 3.2 ounces

- *Ninth week*:
    - The baby's weight increases further and reaches 97 grams or 3.4 ounces

- *Tenth week*:
    - The young marmoset should weigh 103 grams or 3.6 ounces by this point

- *Eleventh week*:
    - The ear tufts start to grow but are dark grey at this stage
    - The benchmark weight at this point is 105 grams or 3.7 ounces

- *Twelfth week*:
    - The young marmoset is not independent and doesn't need to be carried on an adult's back
    - Although it may still be nursing the youngster can also forage for food

- *Fourteenth week*:
    - The young marmoset is no longer nursing
    - A wider area is being explored
    - The ear tufts have grown and turned silvery

- *Seventeenth week*:
  - The baby's weight is now 137 grams or 4.8 ounces

- *Twentieth week*:
  - No longer travels on the adults' back

- *Twenty second week*:
  - The baby's weight reaches 166 grams or 5.8 ounces

- *Twenty eight week*:
  - The ear tufts turn white
  - The weight is now 174 grams or 6.1 ounces

- *Sixtieth week*:
  - The marmoset is now entirely independent
  - Most of the adult teeth have come through.
  - At this age the juvenile is fully sexually mature.

4) Communication between infants & adults

Touch is a crucial part of bonding but communication is just as important for the development and safety of infants and the cohesion and strength of the group overall.

Infant marmosets, like other very young primates (and human babies) have limited vocalisations initially. To begin with, a baby will only produce babbling sounds, which it uses to interact with adults and to attract attention. As the youngster matures, the nature and sophistication of the vocalisations change. Eventually the sounds are the same as those produced by adult marmosets.

5) What to do if a pet marmoset does give birth…

If one has a pet marmoset that becomes pregnant there are things that you need to know:

- If you notice the pregnant marmoset becoming less active it probably means she is a few weeks away from giving birth. However, if the decrease in activity is combined with signs of ill health take her to a vet.

- When she is in labour she should not be disturbed or interfered with. In fact, given marmosets typically give birth during the night and labour only takes about an hour, you may not even know it is happening!

- There is usually only a few minutes between infants and the afterbirth is expelled 10 to 30 minutes after the birth of the last baby. The mother and other troop members usually eat the afterbirth.

- If labour takes longer than an hour, the female appears in distress or extreme pain or the afterbirth is not expelled call a vet!

- As stated, twins are normal for Pygmy Marmosets. If a third baby is born it often dies within the first week.

- If triplets are born it greatly increases the chance that at least one infant will have to be hand-reared as the mother won't be able to adequately feed all three.

- The female will nurse her babies for about 100 days although it may be a shorter period with marmosets in captivity.

- Young are able to begin to eat solid foods when they are about a month old, so hand-rearing goes on for at least that length of time. After 40 days the young can be moved to a mixture of milk substitutes and solids.

6) Why infants are so vulnerable

Infant and baby marmosets are prone to diarrhoea, which is often caused by a bacterial infection. Like all very young animals they can become dehydrated very quickly unless they are treated quickly and effectively. Veterinary treatment will be necessary.

The size of the babies also makes them extremely vulnerable to injury including broken bones. These can be the result of falls out of the nest box of from an adult's back. Owners can also inadvertently injure these babies when they are handling them.

It is strongly suggested that young children should not be allowed to hold or handle infant or even adult marmosets, as children are not always able to judge how tightly they are holding something. 'Loving' a pet can turn to tragedy without the intention to hurt an animal as the bones in these little creatures are tiny.

There are two easy and reliable ways to assess the health of an infant. Firstly, if the tail is curled and pressed against the adult carrying the baby it is doing fine. A limp, straight tail is a very bad sign and indicates that a baby needs to be examined for illness or injury. Secondly, an infant that clings tightly to the top of the adult's back at the shoulder blades is fine. A baby that struggles to hold on and rides below the shoulder blade line is also not doing well.

One shouldn't delay in seeking medical care for an infant because they become very ill very quickly.

7) Hand-rearing information & guidelines

Hand-rearing a tiny, fluffy and extremely cute primate sounds like a fun thing to do. However, it is *extremely* hard work. To do a good job one needs to be committed to spending the time and energy.

It must also be kept in mind that hand-rearing does *not* just refer to feeding an infant. One also has to provide the contact, warmth and emotional security this tiny, vulnerable creature needs. The person who assumes this responsibility has to simulate the natural life of an infant marmoset as closely as possible.

A brooder or something similar to control temperature must be used during the first two weeks, as an infant can't regulate its own body temperature. One can use microwavable heating pads but electric ones are not a good choice; even on the lowest settings they are likely to overheat the marmoset. Too much heat will kill just as surely as cold will.

A new-born must be kept within a specific temperature range: 37.2 – 38.3°C or 99 – 101° F. The baby should feel slightly warm to the touch. If it feels cool it is an indication of hypothermia or abnormally low body temperature. A further sign that he or she is too cold is that the infant will become lethargic.

While using a stuffed toy for the baby to cling to for short periods is an option, it can't under any circumstances replace direct contact from a carer or be used for long periods. All infants need the stimulation – both physical and emotional – of constant contact and affection.

The baby also needs to be carried as motion or movement stimulates the formation of crucial neural pathways. This aids the development of motor skills.

The person hand-rearing a baby marmoset must also help it in the manner its parent would. For instance, the mother or father licks the infant's perineal area to stimulate urination and defecation. A human 'parent' must very gently pat or wipe this area in order to do the same. After three weeks the baby will no longer need this stimulation and should be defecating and urinating spontaneously.

It is important to monitor the baby's weight, starting from birth. Some primate experts suggest weighing an infant daily and in the morning. After the first couple of days there should be steady, small weight gains.

What to feed hand-reared infant Pygmy Marmosets

The first day all these tiny mites should be given is filtered or bottled water with a pinch of glucose in it. Thereafter these babies can be fed commercial baby formula that is used for human infants.

Formulas for premature babies also work very well for infant marmosets, as they are especially high in nutrients. There are also baby formulas for primates that are available in some areas through specialist primate websites and online stores.

The product chosen should have normal iron levels, not additional or supplemental iron. However, if a baby becomes constipated one should change to a low iron formula until the problem is resolved. Gently rubbing baby oil on the anal area can help combat dryness and lubricate the anus a little.

Glucose solution can also help to treat constipation and it can be given to the infant in between feeds. Diarrhoea, on the other hand, can be a sign of lactose intolerance and a vet's advice should be sought in these cases.

While these formulas are available in powdered and liquid form, many primate breeders recommend the powdered form. The liquid has a limited life span and given a marmoset infant ingests tiny amounts at a time there can be a great deal of wastage. The powder allows one to make up formula as it is needed.

The powdered formula should be mixed with filtered water to protect the infant from possible pathogens or chemicals found in tap water. Alternatively, one can use tap water that has been boiled and then allowed to cool. The formula should be heated to 100° F or 37.8° C.

After about three weeks the young start to be interested in solid food. These should be introduced into their diet gradually. One can add human baby products such as strained baby food or baby cereal to the formula.

During weaning one can feed young marmosets many of the same foods that human toddlers are given. If one is unsure about the suitability of a food or brand one can ask for guidance from a vet, breeder or through online forums where marmoset owners offer advice and information in response to questions and problems.

How often to feed infants

The very weak glucose solution should be fed to new-borns every 20 to 30 minutes during the first 24 hours.

Thereafter infants should be fed every 2 hours or on demand and around the clock from day 2 and for the first two weeks of their lives. No, the owner won't get much sleep! Night feeds will fall away after two weeks when the babies begin to sleep through.

The amount given to the marmoset must be gradually and steadily increased. On day 1 the infant should only be given a single drop of solution.

Feeding related tips

Sterilising the feeding syringe

It's important to ensure that the feeding syringe is free of bacteria. Remove the plunger from the syringe and place both items in a container of water. Heat the water in a microwave. Alternatively they can be sterilised in a pot of water heated on a stove top. This should be done both before and after a feed to keep the syringe clean and hygienic.

Warming the feed solution

Just as with human infants the formula must be warmed. The easiest way to do this is to fill the feeding syringe and then stand it in a container of warm or hot (but not boiling) water. The syringe should be removed and shaken from time to time so that the liquid in it heats evenly. You can test the temperature by placing a drop of formula on your wrist. It should be about body temperature.

Additional hand-rearing guidelines

It can be helpful to know what to do, what to look out for and to be prepared for potential problems. While all infants are unique, broadly speaking there are certain aspects they all have in common at various points.

The first 24 hours and week after birth:

- ➢ The infant must be held upright when it is being fed so that there is no risk of choking
- ➢ Don't push the syringe into the infant's mouth as this can cause injuries and / or choking; let the baby find it on its own

- Formula must be squeezed out of a feeding syringe very slowly so the infant can swallow and does not choke

- For the first four days the formula should be diluted. A 50/50 ratio of formula and water is suggested by some breeders

- The syringe, bottle etc. must all be sterilised to remove or at least greatly reduce the risk of bacteria in the food

- Formula and milk should never be reheated

- Mixed, unused formula must be disposed of after 48 hours

- Don't ever miss a scheduled feed

- Don't exceed the amount of food suggested in light of the baby's age and nutritional requirements

- Weak glucose water is a good solution to use in between feeds if a marmoset baby is constipated

- Weigh the baby daily and record the results so progress can be tracked and monitored

- Keep the infant warm at all times but take great care to prevent overheating

- Stimulate the baby to urinate and defecate

- Carry the infant to stimulate neural and motor skill development

- If all is going well an infant will sleep between meals. An infant that moves around, or tries to do so, is in distress of some kind and should be checked

- Diarrhoea in new-borns and infants is a serious problem and must be treated immediately as they dehydrate very quickly. Signs of dehydration include a loss of skin elasticity and sunken eyes

- A small drop of rice or potato water is usually an effective treatment for diarrhoea. Too much of this can, however, cause constipation. If the problem persists seek help from a vet

- At this stage an infant is very fragile and very needy. In addition to regular feeds it requires contact and must be allowed to cling and be carried around as much as possible.

- Ensure that babies are kept out of drafts and away from animals and – even more importantly – from people that are sick or have cold sores

The second week:

- The infant must be held upright or placed on its tummy when it is being fed so that it doesn't choke

- By now the youngster knows when it has had enough food and will turn its head away

- Weigh the baby daily and record the results so progress can be tracked and monitored

- Keep the infant warm and prevent overheating

- Stimulate the baby to urinate and defecate even if it has started doing so spontaneously

- Carry the infant as much as possible to stimulate neural and motor skill development

- The baby still sleeps a great deal but less than initially

- Crawling at this point is a developmental milestone and not necessarily a sign of problems. Check the body temperature to make sure

- It can be introduced to the adult marmosets at this age. However, some adults may be aggressive so one needs to monitor the situation very closely. An adult can kill a baby with ease

- Signs of health include a tight grip when clinging, a curled tail, steady weigh gain and stools that are putty-like in consistency

- Tummy problems, excessive scratching, sneezing or laboured breathing must all be addressed, as they are signs of ill health or an environmental problem. For example, sometimes breathing difficulties are due to a lack of humidity which can be solved by using a humidifier in the room the baby spends time in.

The third week:

> ➢ Vitamin D3 should be added to the formula mixture (sneezing can be a sign of a D3 deficiency)

> ➢ In addition to eating more, babies at this age also take longer to eat

> ➢ At this stage urination and defecation should be spontaneous. If there are concerns one can continue to stimulate the perineal area

> ➢ The periods of being awake are even longer

> ➢ The baby at this point is far more interested in the world around it – including in its owner – and starts to grab and hold things

> ➢ Interaction between these babies, humans and other marmosets is more focused and dynamic

> ➢ Play will begin to emerge and the need for interaction, toys and stimulation increases greatly. These young marmosets become very distressed and even fearful when left alone

> ➢ Continue to weigh the baby daily and record the results so progress can be tracked and monitored

> ➢ Go on keeping the youngster warm.

The fourth week:

> ➢ Provide as much contact with adult and juvenile marmosets as possible

> ➢ Don't leave a young Finger Monkey alone as they become fearful, anxious and agitated. At this point their need for companionship and contact is constant

> ➢ D3 should be given twice a week

➤ Feeding has become less frequent and new foods and textures can be introduced. For example, one can provide foods such as yoghurt or baby food as young this age can lick and lap

➤ Weigh the baby daily and record the results so progress can be tracked and monitored

➤ Continue to keep the infant warm

➤ It should no longer be necessary to stimulate the baby to urinate and defecate as it should be entirely spontaneous at this stage

➤ Continue to carry the infant to stimulate neural and motor skill development

➤ Overall levels of activity and playfulness continue to increase

The fifth and sixth weeks:

➤ At this age Pygmy Marmosets begin to feed themselves so food should be left in bowls for them

➤ Be prepared for a great deal of mess while he or she learns. Eventually more food will end up in the little one's tummy than all over their bedding box

➤ They become increasingly interested in trying new foods and will feed from their owner's hand (or even mouth!)

➤ Although they still sleep a fair amount, they are *very* active and demanding when awake. If they don't get the social interaction they need they will demand it very loudly

➤ Supply them with toys and safe things to climb so they can further improve and develop their motor and cognitive skills

➤ Allow them to spend a significant amount of time each day with the adult and juvenile marmosets. If there aren't any then the owner is *everything*!

➤ They mustn't be on their own except for short periods. They don't outgrow needing companionship... ever.

The tenth week:

The hand rearing is now over although it can be hard to persuade the juvenile of this! He or she may cling to the human carer and call to be let back out.

However, you must harden your heart and leave the youngster with the marmoset troop who will take over his or her continued education.

After a short period the juvenile should settle completely. The owner must monitor the situation regularly though to ensure there is no aggression shown towards the newcomer by the adults or the other juveniles and that he or she continues to thrive.

Feeding, appearance, weight and behaviour all need to be watched as they are good indicators of whether or not the new arrival is happy and healthy.

Chapter 10: Costs & where to buy a marmoset

While Pygmy Marmosets are increasingly popular as pets they are still not all that easy to come by, especially legally! The relative scarcity combined with the high demand means that these tiny critters come with a hefty price tag.

1) Costs

At time of writing the purchase price for a baby Finger or Pocket Monkey from a reputable, registered breeder is $3,000 to $3,900 or £2,310 to £3,010. If someone is offering babies at far lower prices it's likely to be a scam or a form of illegal trade.

One-off items and expenses

While this is not an exhaustive list, you will need to invest in the following items:

- Enclosure or cage (building or purchasing)
- Nesting box
- Substrate
- Plants and branches
- Full-spectrum fluorescent lights
- Blankets or towels for inside the nesting boxes
- Feeding syringe(s)
- Food and water bowls
- Feeding bottles and / or sipper tubes and bottles
- An implement suitable for cleaning out the substrate
- Humidifier
- Heat lamps
- Thermometer to monitor the temperature in the habitat
- Hygrometer to monitor the humidity in the habitat
- Toys.

Some of these items like blankets will need to be replaced as they become worn or are no longer hygienic. Other items are much harder wearing and will not need replacing for quite some time.

Ongoing expenses

You will also have to budget for the following:

- Nappies
- Hand sanitiser
- Substrate
- Replacement blankets or towels
- Annual vet check-up
- Food
- Replacement plants and branches
- Replacement or additional toys
- Supplements
- Maintenance costs for the cage or enclosure.

Keep in mind that the lighting and heating these little primates require will add to utility costs on an ongoing basis. All of these expenses will be there for the duration of the primate's life.

Over and above these financial costs are the less tangible and quantifiable ones: the huge amounts of time and energy an owner must spend and expend caring for these little primates.

2) Where you can buy a Pygmy Marmoset

One can buy marmosets from breeders and online. One can also sometimes adopt a marmoset from a sanctuary or rescue organisation although this does not happen often.

However, there are a number of things that you must keep in mind so that you doesn't inadvertently participate in illegal or black market dealings or fall victim to one of the numerous scams on the Internet.

Breeders

There are a number of breeders, both registered and unregistered, that advertise themselves and their Marmosets but how do you know if it is a breeder that is entirely trustworthy? One option is that you can visit the websites of marmoset or primate sanctuaries or associations to see if the breeder is listed or registered with them. The second option is to ask the breeder for proof of registration.

In the US a breeder must have a United States Department of Agriculture (USDA) license. The breeder must be prepared to provide a copy of his or her license or at least the number. A refusal to do so is a bad sign and a potential buyer should make enquiries with the USDA and, if necessary, report the breeder.

Certain US states require both breeders and owners to hold permits. A permit, called a Captive Bred Wildlife (CBW) permit, is also necessary when transporting a marmoset across state lines. In other states private ownership of primates is illegal. A US resident considering buying a Pygmy Marmoset must enquire about legal requirements before making a purchase.

In the UK one does not require a license or permit to own or breed primates of any kind including these marmosets. However, this situation is not without its critics. The Royal Society for the Prevention of Cruelty to Animals (RSPCA) doesn't mince their words at all.

On their website they state that they are opposed to keeping primates as pets because they are highly intelligent and have complex needs that can't be met in a home environment. At time of writing they are calling for a national ban on both trading and ownership. Their motive is to prevent primates suffering in the unnatural conditions they are in when kept as pets.

Of course if one is looking for a pet you may not really be concerned about having the 'right' paperwork to show that a breeder is registered. Your concerns will probably be that the pet is healthy and socialised.

If a breeder won't or can't provide medical records such as proof of vaccinations, worry. If a breeder won't allow you to have a vet examine an animal, go somewhere else. If a seller won't meet in person or talk over the phone, be suspicious. Be cautious about pets up for adoption as there is likely to be an underlying health or behaviour problem or the animal may have been illegally obtained by the seller.

Some breeders will offer more general health guarantees that offer protection against congenital health problems or severe behavioural problems. In these situations, the breeder may agree to take the marmoset back. Legitimate breeders will sell a baby and provide:

- A Health Certificate issued by a qualified vet
- USDA paperwork if the breeder is in the US
- A brochure or pamphlet giving basic care information. Others sell books or e-Books
- Access to advice and guidance via telephone or email. Some breeders offer a 24-hour helpline.

Don't be blinded by how sweet and cute these tiny primates are. Don't allow a breeder to rush you or get pushy. Take your time. Ask someone with more knowledge to help you decide if you are still inexperienced. If properly cared for, a marmoset will be part of your life for several decades. Make sure you are right for each other.

Scams and illegal trading

An assumption that is safe to make is that a very cheap Pygmy Marmoset or a deal where one only has to pay for shipping is either an illegal trade or an out-and-out scam. Exotic pets are very expensive so a 'cheap' one is bound to generate suspicion.

There are shameless individuals out there. This link is (not surprisingly) no longer available but it makes the mind boggle:

Real Live Potty-Trained Finger Monkey for just $2!

Decorate your digits with the newest fad in fashion: Finger monkeys! These potty-trained creatures (all you need is a houseplant!) are economically friendly: on average, finger monkeys eat just one Trix banana per day and require little to no upkeep, save for a daily tickle on their belly. Each monkey comes with a pre-trained special trick.

Offer's Fine Print:
* No limit - Buy as many as you'd like
* Poachers are forbidden to purchase.

There are just so many problems with this! It is factually incorrect and therefore misleading. Anybody who bought a Pygmy Marmoset expecting it to be toilet trained, eat almost nothing, live in a pot plant, etc. is in for a very rude awakening. These are in all likelihood the pet owners who neglect and abandon animals.

It is also morally utterly reprehensible to sell living, feeling and thinking creatures as accessories! One is no doubt supposed to believe that this is an ethical business because they don't sell to poachers.

Chapter 11: Conclusion

A Pygmy Marmoset is a demanding pet and companion that many consider to be far from ideal. While they will certainly entertain you, they need – constantly – a great deal from you in return.

As a loving and responsible primate owner you will have to make sure that your marmoset has all that it requires in order to be healthy and happy. The full range of its physical, emotional, intellectual and social needs must be met.

Their physical and emotional requirements include a good, healthy diet; a stimulating, spacious environment; the company of their own kind and annual vet check-ups and care.

These little primates need daily handling, affectionate interaction with their owners and play time. You need to provide objects they can safely play and interact with that provide fun and the mental stimulation these intelligent creatures must have in order to be happy.

1) Safety tips

As a marmoset owner one has a duty of care. This involves both keeping it happy *and* protecting it from harm. While nobody can guard against every threat and eventuality there are certain things you can do:

o   Ensure that the enclosure or cage is secure so that the marmosets can't get out and no would-be predators can get in. this includes domestic dogs and cats who will think a Pygmy Marmoset is a little snack!

o   If a marmoset will be roaming the house ensure that all the doors and windows are kept closed and ensure family members know not to open them

o   Don't have plants toxic to marmosets anywhere they can get to them o Don't allow a pet marmoset to sleep in or on the bed; there is a good chance that you could accidentally roll onto, hit or kick it. Given the size of these primates that could result in severe injury or death

o Don't allow very young children to handle marmosets and older children must be taught how to do so gently and safely.

2) Care schedule

Looking after a primate is a daunting responsibility. What may make it less intimidating and easier is to break tasks down.

Daily tasks

- Feed pet marmosets as often in the day as their age requires
- Monitor the weight of infant and baby marmosets
- Observe pet(s) for any changes in behaviour or signs of illness
- Clean out water containers and refill them with clean water
- Remove faecal matter from the substrate
- Spend some time bonding.

Weekly tasks

- Clean water containers and refill them
- Clean and disinfect the cage or enclosure
- Replace the substrate if necessary
- Move some branches or other décor items around to increase the stimulation
- Introduce additional foliage if necessary.

Annual tasks

- Schedule an appointment with a primate vet for an annual check up
- Perform maintenance work on the cage or enclosure.

3) Do's… in no particular order

- ✓ Learn about marmosets in general and Pygmy Marmosets in particular. Buy books, watch videos, talk to experts or attend a course at a marmoset or primate sanctuary.

- ✓ Join a primate or marmoset online group; the articles and forums are a very valuable source of information and support.

- ✓ Find a vet that can treat and handle a tiny primate.

- ✓ Invest in *at least* two marmosets so they can keep each other company. This is essential, not a nice-to-have.

- ✓ Take the time to bond with your pet and to get to know it really well in terms of both personality and behaviour.

- ✓ Make sure that the cage or enclosure is clean and hygienic, pest-free and replicates their natural habitat as closely as possible.

- ✓ Keep the cage or enclosure pest-free as they, especially cockroaches, pose a serious health threat to this species.

- ✓ Ensure your tiny primates have ongoing mental stimulation.

- ✓ Ensure your pet receives all the necessary preventative vet care and regular check-ups.

- ✓ If you don't want to breed – and it is not recommended –obtain contraceptives from the vet.

- ✓ Take steps to keep ticks, fleas, etc. away.

- ✓ Feed your primate the right diet and always supply fresh, clean water.

- ✓ Keep a primate First Aid Kit and contact list handy.

4) Don'ts… in no particular order

- ▪ Leave a Pygmy Marmoset alone for extended periods.

- Have only one marmoset.

- Neglect annual vet check-ups.

- Provide insufficient space or stimulation for these very active and intelligent little creatures.

- Ignore changes in behaviour and appearance that may indicate illness or distress.

- Feed inappropriate or non-nutritious foods that lead to malnourishment or obesity.

- Neglect cleaning tasks so that a cage or enclosure becomes dirty and unhygienic.

- Allow a marmoset the run of the house unsupervised.

- Feed a diet that lacks variety.

- Allow anybody who is sick to go near or to handle a marmoset.

- Punish a marmoset for defecating or biting; they are simply being a primate.

- This must be stated again: don't have only one marmoset.

- Neglect bites or scratches from a marmoset

- Don't believe everything you read on the Internet. There is a lot of inaccurate information out there so one needs to cross check or consult an expert.

And don't join the ranks of those who have abandoned a pet Pygmy Marmoset because they:

- Are noisy
- Are demanding
- Make a mess with their food
- Can't be house trained
- Urinate and defecate wherever they are
- Are fairly good at getting out of a nappy
- Don't listen

- Can be smelly
- Have been known to masturbate
- Bite
- Cost a lot
- Can be destructive
- Use urine to mark territory

The reason that all of these are unacceptable reasons to give up on, abandon, re-sell or give away a Pygmy Marmoset is that all of these are natural behaviours that an owner should have known about or found out about before he or she bought one of these primates!

These are wild animals, not domesticated pets, and can't be expected to change their nature.

But if one really can't keep a Pygmy Marmoset for genuinely unavoidable and unforeseen reasons then one should approach an official primate rescue and re-homing organisation rather than sell or give a primate to an individual you knows nothing about.

Sanctuaries and rescue organisations are committed to the long-term wellbeing of the primates in their care. They will all have limitations in terms of how many animals they can house at any given time but are often able to refer one to another organisation if they can't assist.

Because they are specialised organisations they will have knowledge of exactly what each primate species requires to be healthy and happy. The staff at these facilities do all they can to help marmosets adapt to their new surroundings and deal with the stress that goes with it. This can take quite some time as these little creatures are territorial and may also have imprinted on their owner. Being separated and relocated is very hard for them!

5) *And from the point of view of the pet…*

- *I need you for everything and I always will.*

- *I am utterly dependent on you for my food, my home and help when I get sick.*

- *I require your time, attention and understanding.*

- *I need you to appreciate that I'm not a domestic pet. I won't come when you call me, do tricks or stop the behaviours natural to my species.*

- *Don't stop loving me and caring for me when I'm an adult and not as cute.*

- *I won't understand what you want from me.*

- *I'm a wild animal; the concepts of 'good' and 'bad' don't mean anything to me.*

- *I won't understand why I'm being hurt or punished. All that will teach me is fear and destroy my trust in you. And I will remember the pain.*

- *Biting is normal behaviour to me and I don't usually mean to hurt you.*

- *I may not understand the words but talk to me but I like the sound of your voice and its part of making me feel safe.*

- *Remember how tiny and fragile I am. I can be injured very easily so treat me with gentleness.*

- *Don't abandon me when I get sick or old; I need you even more then.*

- *Comfort me when I'm sick or frightened.*

6) And in closing...

There is no doubt that Pygmy Marmosets are cute, very smart and fun to watch. However, they are not a wise choice for a pet owner who has never owned a primate or monkey before. Most primate experts go out of their way to discourage ownership of these tiny primates by unexperienced individuals.

Owning any pet is a responsibility and a commitment. One can't give them back or get rid of them because they are no longer cute or fun! With marmosets it is a long-term commitment given their longevity. Their environmental, dietary and social requirements also mean that they are costly pets.

Finally, before buying a marmoset (or any primate) it is essential to check on the local requirements in terms of the need for a permit or license of some kind. An illegal animal is in danger of being confiscated and the owner faces a potential fine.

This guide's primary purpose is to make sure that you have the information that you need to decide, first and foremost, if this is *really* the right pet for you, for your spouse, for your child or for your lifestyle.

If the answer is a confident and honest "Yes" in spite of all the demands, challenges and expenses involved, this pet owner's guide will give you the details that will help you to keep your Pygmy Marmosets (please note the deliberate use of the plural) healthy and happy.

If you are one of those individuals who truly commits to owning and caring for one of these amazing little primates you will be rewarded by having a pet that is smart, full of beans, entertaining and has loads of personality!

Enjoy your Pygmy Marmosets and teach others about this amazing species!

Published by IMB Publishing 2017

Printed in Great Britain
by Amazon

27184867R00066